BERTIE COUNTY
A Brief History

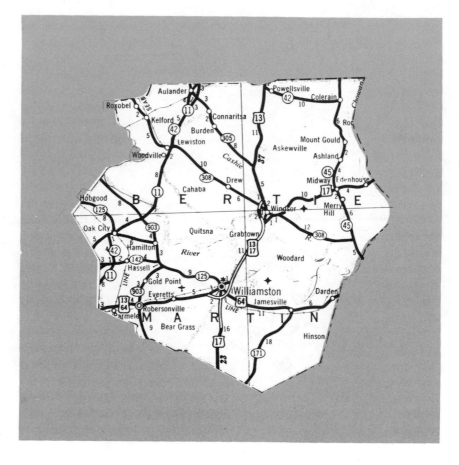

BERTIE COUNTY

A Brief History

by

Alan D. Watson

Raleigh
North Carolina Department of Cultural Resources
Division of Archives and History
1982

DEPARTMENT OF CULTURAL RESOURCES

Sara W. Hodgkins
Secretary

DIVISION OF ARCHIVES AND HISTORY

William S. Price, Jr.
Director

Copyright, 1982, by the North Carolina Division of Archives and History
(ISBN 0-86526-194-6)

TABLE OF CONTENTS

ILLUSTRATIONS

FOREWORD

In 1963, when the State Department of Archives and History published a brief history of Lenoir County, it was hoped that funding would be forthcoming whereby comparable histories could be produced for the remaining ninety-nine counties. Nearly two decades later, the project has barely been started; only seven county histories have been published to date: Burke, Dare, Davie, Edgecombe, New Hanover, and Rowan in addition to Lenoir. Failure to publish these brief surveys has been caused by lack of funding for printing and the difficulty of finding competent writers who have time to carry through with the production of quality manuscripts.

The Division of Archives and History, North Carolina Department of Cultural Resources, has been fortunate in two respects. The authors who have written the pamphlets published since the early 1960s have been well versed in their subjects and have produced readable and reliable studies. And thanks to grants from the Smith Richardson Foundation, Inc., and the North Carolina Bicentennial Local History Fund, with complementary approval by the Davie County Bicentennial Committee, supplemented by state funds, it has been possible to proceed on a limited scale with the publication of county histories.

The division is particularly fortunate to have obtained the services of Alan D. Watson, professor of history at the University of North Carolina at Wilmington, to write *Bertie County: A Brief History*. The author of the Edgecombe County history, Dr. Watson also wrote *Society in Colonial North Carolina* and *Money and Monetary Problems in Early North Carolina*, both published by the division. He is a regular contributor to the *North Carolina Historical Review* and other scholarly journals. His history of Bertie will interest readers, because he relates many human-interest incidents as he tells the history of that eastern county.

The manuscript was edited and seen through the press by Jeffrey J. Crow. Dr. Crow is historical publications editor II and head of the General Publications Branch of the Historical Publications Section, Division of Archives and History. The pamphlet was proofread by Patricia R. Johnson, a member of the section's staff.

Memory F. Mitchell
Historical Publications Administrator

August 1, 1981

INTRODUCTION

Bertie County, located in the northeastern Coastal Plain of North Carolina, displays a topography of low, gently rolling land that encompasses 721 square miles, 5 percent of which is covered by water. Fertile uplands and lowlands accompanied by large swamps called pocosins combine to render the economy of the county primarily agricultural. The Chowan and Roanoke rivers, which border Bertie, and the Cashie River, which intersects the county, provided needed transportation facilities during the early years of settlement and fostered as well substantial and ongoing fishing enterprises. A few small towns and a bustling county seat, Windsor, along with scattered small industry interrupt an otherwise thoroughly rural atmosphere.

The modern history of Bertie County dates from explorations of the area conducted by the colonists of Sir Walter Raleigh's first expedition in 1585-1586, but the English tramped upon ground that had long been inhabited by the natives of North America. At least three large Indian town sites that served an aboriginal populace 2,000 to 5,000 years ago have been discovered in the county. Moratuck, on the Roanoke River about seven miles south of Windsor, Tandequemuc, slightly east of Sans Souci Ferry on the Cashie River, and Metpcuuem, on the Chowan River at the mouth of Salmon Creek, contained people who supported themselves by fishing, farming, and hunting with crude wood and stone tools.

The well-drained, easily cultivated lands in the county continued to appeal to native inhabitants, so that the English in the late sixteenth century encountered several Indian tribes in the vicinity of what became Bertie County. The largest was the Tuscarora, an Iroquoian group who separated from the Five Nations Confederation in New England and occupied the area stretching from the upper Neuse to the Roanoke River. Along the Roanoke River was the Meherrin tribe, also Iroquois, and extending southward were members of small, disparate Algonquian tribes. Making frequent appearances for purposes of hunting and raiding were the Catawba, a Siouan tribe to the west, the Shawnee from the north, and members of the Five Nations.

With the appearance of Raleigh's colonists the relatively halcyon days of Indian existence along the Atlantic coast concluded quickly as the Europeans began their inexorable drive to dispossess the American aboriginals. England, of course, waited until 1607 and the settlement at Jamestown to establish its first permanent colony in the New World. Despite the Heath Patent of 1629 that bestowed Carolana, later Carolina, upon Sir Robert Heath, the Virginians treated the area as their southern frontier until the eight Lords Proprietors established their superior claim to the land by the royal grants in 1663 and 1665.

From exploratory parties seeking the whereabouts of the Lost Colony, Virginians gained knowledge of the fertile lands to the south of their province. John Pory in 1622 led a well-publicized expedition to "South Virginia" or the "Southern Plantations" as the Albemarle region was called. During the next three decades hunters, trappers, and explorers from Virginia traveled to the area and undoubtedly viewed the terrain of modern Bertie on occasion. In 1650 Edward Bland, a Virginia merchant, organized an expedition that explored west of the Chowan River and as far south as the Roanoke River.

Virginia interest in North Carolina culminated in 1655 with the appearance of Nathaniell Batts, an Indian trader who represented the interests of Francis Yeardley, son of a Virginia governor. The Nicholas Cumberford map of 1657 shows Batts's residence, a 20-foot-square building with two rooms and a chimney, at the mouth of Salmon Creek in what became Bertie County. Although he may not have been the first permanent settler in North Carolina, according to historian Lindley S. Butler, Batts "is gratefully remembered by North Carolina as its first citizen and an important founder of the colony. . . ." Following Batts, between 1658 and 1661, numerous Virginians from Surry, Isle of Wight, Nansemond, and Norfolk counties moved into the Albemarle region, creating a society on the southern fringe of Virginia even before Charles II of England granted Carolina to the Lords Proprietors in 1663.

After the Carolina grant the area that became Bertie was part of Chowan Precinct, which in turn helped to form Albemarle County as Virginians continued to move into Carolina. The lower part of the Bertie peninsula, at the mouth of Salmon Creek, filled so quickly that the proprietors designated it as one of the three ports of entry for the colony in 1676. The rapid influx of people, coupled with poor proprietary governance, resulted in internal dissension that occasionally erupted in full-scale rebellion. At the same time white expansion angered the Indians, producing conflict that threatened the existence of the colony early in the eighteenth century.

During the course of the turbulent proprietary era several provincial governors resided on Bertie soil. One of the most notorious, Seth Sothel, owned a plantation on Salmon Creek. Appointed governor in 1678, Sothel was captured by Algerian pirates and ransomed before finally arriving in North Carolina in 1682. However, his despotic rule produced a rebellion in 1689 during which Sothel was imprisoned and subsequently banished from the government.

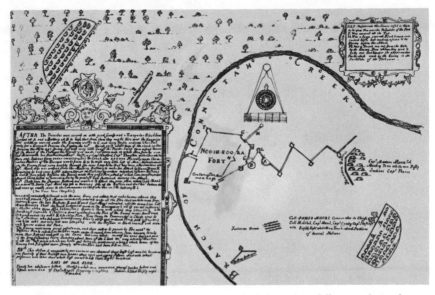

In November, 1712, Colonel James Moore marched thirty-three fellow South Carolinians and nearly 1,000 Indian allies northward to help subdue the Tuscarora uprising. On March 20, 1713, he launched a general assault on the Tuscarora fort of Nohoroco in present Greene County; the three-day battle forever ended Tuscarora strength in North Carolina. Seen here is Moore's map of the Indian camp. (Photographs from the files of the North Carolina Division of Archives and History unless otherwise specified.)

Another of the executives who lived in Bertie was Edward Hyde, a distant cousin of Queen Anne I, who arrived in 1710 to serve a two-year, stormy tenure. Although he ended the civil conflict known as Cary's Rebellion in 1711, he witnessed the outbreak of the Tuscarora Indian War, which devastated the province. While the war was in progress, Hyde became the first governor of North Carolina when the colony was officially separated from South Carolina in 1712. During the same year, however, Hyde fell victim to a yellow fever epidemic.

Succeeding Hyde was Thomas Pollock of Bal Gra plantation overlooking Salmon Creek. One of the wealthiest men in the province and a member of the governor's council, Pollock was chosen by his fellow councillors to act as governor upon the death of Hyde. Among other factors, Pollock's friendship and influence with a Tuscarora chieftain, Thomas Blunt, caused the segment of the Tuscarora along the Roanoke River to remain neutral in the Indian war. Although Pollock was relieved of the duties of governor with the appearance of Charles Eden in 1714, he again became the acting executive at Eden's death in 1722. Pollock's second term was brief, for he died five months later in the same year.

3

When Charles Eden became governor in 1714, North Carolina had concluded the Tuscarora Indian War and entered into a period of "peace and quietness." During Eden's tenure the Tuscarora who chose to remain in the colony rather than join their Iroquois kinsmen in New York were placed on a reservation along the Roanoke River in what later became Bertie County. The governor, known for his probable association with pirates, particularly Blackbeard, who plagued the coastal waters, made his home at Eden House, a plantation overlooking the Chowan River. Subsequently, royal governor Gabriel Johnston, who married Penelope, the stepdaughter of Eden, resided at Eden House, which became the nucleus of a small community in the county.

THE PEOPLE OF BERTIE

After the conclusion of the Tuscarora Indian War the western half of Chowan Precinct underwent a population boom. Fertile land and easy access provided by numerous rivers and streams enticed settlers to the area that had been vacated by the defeated Indians. In order to satisfy the need of the new residents for proximate local government the provincial assembly in 1722 divided Chowan to create Bertie Precinct (later County). The eponym derived from the name of James and probably Henry Bertie, brothers and proprietors of Carolina.

Bertie County in turn spawned all or part of four additional counties. Governor George Burrington remarked in 1731 that Bertie was "a very thriveing Place which is so much increased that there is talk already of a new division in it." Actually, some of its land had been used in 1729 to form Tyrrell. By 1741 the extensive area and burgeoning population of Bertie resulted in the formal creation of Edgecombe (which had existed in legal limbo since 1732) and Northampton counties solely from Bertie. And in 1759 the legislature further reduced the size of Bertie to help establish Hertford County, though the vague boundary between Bertie and Hertford was not properly settled until 1907.

At mid-eighteenth century Bertie was one of the most populous counties in the province despite the loss of land that comprised Edgecombe and Northampton counties. Its families, averaging 8.7 persons, exceeded in size those found in other eastern North Carolina counties. A 1755 list of taxables (white males at least sixteen years of age and all blacks at least twelve years of age) showed that Bertie's taxable population was surpassed only by those of Edgecombe and Craven counties. A decade later the rapid growth of the backcountry contributed to a drastic decline in Bertie's relative population ranking. In 1766 nine counties reported more taxables than Bertie. However, by 1790 the division of the western counties and emigration from the state vaulted Bertie into a position of preeminence, for only Rowan and Halifax counties contained more people than Bertie according to the first federal census.

Contributing to the growing population of Bertie in the eighteenth century was the steadily increasing number of Negro slaves. Africans undoubtedly appeared early in the settlement of the Albemarle as Virginians brought their bondsmen with them. By the early 1700s slaves were imported directly into North Carolina. In the 1740s Negroes constituted one fourth of the population of Bertie, and by some accounts a most dangerous quarter of the people. Caesar, a slave belonging to James

Parker, was executed about 1762 for the murder of his master. Four years later Moses and Toddy, slaves owned by Cullen Pollock, were hanged for unspecified crimes.

Despite the restiveness of the slave populace as witnessed by their continuous acts of resistance and running away, the institution of slavery became progressively more entrenched in Bertie. The number of households containing bondsmen rose from 17 percent in 1751 to 43 percent in 1774. In addition, the percentage of families listing one to four slave taxables declined markedly while the percentage owning five to nine increased significantly. On the eve of the Revolution over a third of the slave-owning families possessed at least five black taxables, headed by Dr. Robert Lenox, who listed thirty-three slave taxables in 1774.

Occupying an anomalous position in a society dominated by whites and Negro bondsmen were the free nonwhites, variously called blacks and mulattoes. Originating from slaves freed for meritorious services or from humanitarian concerns, from runaway slaves who successfully passed as free persons, and from miscegenation in which the mother (white or black) was free, the free Negroes approximated 2 to 3 percent of the taxable population of Bertie before the Revolution. County tax lists recorded 37 free Negroes in 1751, 48 in 1763, and 59 in 1774.

The free Negroes suffered numerous discriminations, both legal and illegal. They shouldered a more onerous tax burden by having to pay levies for their wives and all children over twelve years of age, unlike whites whose female family members were untaxed and whose males were taxed only at age sixteen. Several justices of the peace in Bertie gained a notorious reputation in the 1730s for apprenticing free Negro orphans to longer terms than permitted by law, conduct so flagrant that the legislature finally took action in order "that such an illegal practice may be exploded." And there was always the frightening possibility of being sold into slavery, particularly if a free Negro could not produce proper identification and proof of his or her status.

Sharing Bertie in the eighteenth century with those of European and African origins was a remnant of the aboriginal population—the Tuscarora Indians. After their defeat in the Tuscarora Indian War most of the Tuscarora left North Carolina to join the Five (Iroquois) Nations in New York, producing, in effect, the Six Nations confederation. Those who remained in North Carolina were moved to a reservation created by the governor and council in 1717. Bounded by the Roanoke River and Roquist Creek, the reservation contained some of the more fertile land of the county, and it was not long before whites began to encroach upon the territory. As early as 1721 interlopers threatened to "create Feuds and disturbances" among the Indians. By 1748 continuing friction prompted the assembly to pass legislation to define more exactly the boundaries of the Indians' land.

Reservation life for King Tom Blunt, the Tuscarora chieftain, and the approximately 800 Indians who settled in Bertie proved a difficult, sometimes intolerable, adjustment. Confinement, enticement by other Indians, and insults by white neighbors resulted in the rapid decline of the numbers under Blunt's command. In addition to trying to engross reservation land, whites contributed to the dissatisfaction and eventual demise of the Tuscarora by selling them strong drink, refusing them ferriage privileges, and hailing them into court for various offenses ranging from nonpayment of debt to harboring fugitive slaves. Disenchantment with reservation life was so great that by 1731 only about 600 Tuscarora remained in Bertie.

When North Carolina secured an enumeration of the white and Indian population in 1754 for purposes of determining the manpower of the province in the face of an impending war with the French, Governor Arthur Dobbs reported only 301 Tuscarora—100 men and 201 women and children. Moravian Bishop August Spangenberg, who traveled through the county in 1752, was taken to the reservation by Thomas Whitmell, a former trader with the Indians but then "one of the richest men in the neighborhood." Spangenberg reported that the Indians had a tract of "good land." However, they were few in number, lived in poverty, and were oppressed by the whites.

In the 1760s most of the Tuscarora left North Carolina to join the Six Nations in New York. A Tuscarora chieftain from that area visited North Carolina in 1766 to make arrangements with Governor William Tryon for the removal of those who desired to leave the province. In return for a 150-year lease on approximately 8,000 acres of reservation land (confirmed by the assembly in December, 1766), Robert Jones, William Williams, and Thomas Pugh advanced the Indians sufficient money to finance their journey northward. About 155 Tuscarora left in August, 1766, leaving approximately a hundred older Indians on the remainder of the reservation.

Left with about half the land allotted to them by the law of 1748, the remaining Tuscarora sought the protection of Governor William Tryon. When offering the governor deerskins as a token of their loyalty, representatives of the tribe pleaded poverty as an excuse for the meager gift. They claimed that by education and custom they were "unable to acquire a livelihood otherwise than by hunting," but "ill natured persons" frequently appropriated and destroyed their guns and even whipped them "for pursuing game on their Land."

During the Revolution whites took advantage of the general animosity

By the time the last of the Tuscarora Indians left North Carolina for New York in 1803, most of their lands in Bertie County had been confiscated or purportedly leased by unscrupulous whites. This survey of the Tuscarora reservation was made for the General Assembly on June 17, 1803.

toward Indians and the disorganized nature of the state government to deprive the Tuscarora of most of their remaining land, despite the protective law of 1748. Between 1775 and 1777 all but a small portion of the reservation was seized by means of long-term leases that called for a pittance of compensation. Not until December, 1777, did the House of Commons recognize the injustice to the Indians by prohibiting further entries in the Tuscarora lands and appointing a commission to superintend Indian affairs. Legislation the following year confirmed the action of the lower house but legalized the leases.

Finding little sympathy among the white populace and having their lands taken in such callous fashion, the aged, dwindling remnant of the Tuscarora soon proved ready to move northward. In 1801 a Tuscarora delegation from New York visited Governor Benjamin Williams in Raleigh to advise him that the North Carolina Tuscarora wished to depart the state. Legislation in 1802 complied with the desires of the Indians, allowing them to lease their undevised lands and providing that all leases would revert to the state. The statute also created a commission to represent the interests of the Indians in the state.

In June, 1803, the last of the Tuscarora departed North Carolina, leaving in their wake former reservation land, or the Indian Woods area, to the whites, a number of mixed-blooded people, and rich stores of tales and traditions. A report of the commission in the same year revealed the swindle of the Indians. The 1766 lease and subsequent land deals, represented as slightly more than 18,000 acres, actually amounted to over 58,000 acres, leaving the Tuscarora 2,916 acres. The remaining land brought more than $20,000 at public auction, which was used to buy horses and supplies for the trek to New York and to purchase land in New York for their settlement. In 1831 by a deed written in Niagara County, New York, seven Tuscarora chiefs sold to the people of North Carolina all their rights to the land in Bertie County.

After the first federal census Bertie's population declined for three decades and did not again reach the 1790 total until 1850. Poverty, the stifling effect of one-party politics, and cultural stagnation—or so it seemed—early in the nineteenth century began to gain North Carolina the nickname of the "Rip Van Winkle" state and prompted the outmigration of large numbers of enterprising whites who sought more promising futures in the Old Northwest or along the Gulf Coast. In 1830 the number of white residents in Bertie, 5,258, represented a 26-percent dip from the figure in 1790.

Representative of those who departed Bertie was George W. Cooper, who in 1836 became a resident of Yazoo County, Mississippi. Reminiscing, Cooper said that he did not seek the pleasures that his "old state used to afford," but he sometimes wished to return to the Cashie meeting-house, hear the preacher, meet old acquaintances, and see "the Girles all dressed in their best," perhaps even putting his "potato grabbers on some of them at the risk of the fire of pistol or the point of Bowey Knife." Nonetheless, he attempted to persuade his correspondent, young Thomas Heckstall of Bertie, that the healthfulness of the climate and the fertility of the soil in Mississippi merited a departure from North Carolina.

In some instances those who remained behind the western exodus regretted their circumstances. Ann Maria Rhodes, sister of Jonathan T. Jacocks, who had moved to Tennessee, wrote a plaintive letter to her brother in 1826. She noted that some Windsor men were also considering moving to Tennessee but that their wives objected to the proposed change. For her part, Ann Rhodes would have gone "with pleasure" and would have been "proud to leave this poor miserable dirty hole for . . . she despise[d] the very name of Windsor."

Her bitterness might well have derived from the ill health of her immediate family and the enmity of relatives. She had just lost an infant daughter to "dropsy of the brain," her mother probably had malaria, one of her two boys was "a poor sickly fellow," her husband's health was "not very good," and she had not been well for several months. Compounding her difficulties were her family's recent resettlement in Windsor after spending some time in New York and lawsuits that had been lodged by relatives in Bertie County against her mother.

Compensating for the emigration of whites from Bertie was the steadily increasing number of Negroes, principally slaves, in the years between the Revolution and the Civil War. Although whites slightly outnumbered blacks according to the first federal census, by 1800 the black inhabitants of the county comprised the majority of the population, and for the next 170 years accounted for 55.3 to 59.9 percent of the county's residents. Slaves in 1790 appeared in 43 percent of the Bertie households (including those of nonresidents), averaging 8.3 per slave-owning family. Whitmell Hill and John Lenox, reporting 130 and 91 slaves respectively, were the largest slaveholders.

After the Revolution the social conflict and disorder that had characterized the war "generated powerful internal tensions that racially destabilized southern society, particularly North Carolina," according to historian Jeffrey J. Crow. The realization of freedom by many slaves during the Revolution, the libertarian philosophy of the movement, and the West Indian slave insurrections at the end of the eighteenth century caused continued unrest among bondsmen while promoting fear in a white populace already beset by poverty and political divisiveness. Ex-

10

acerbating those conditions was the Second Great Awakening, a nation-wide religious revival affecting North Carolina by 1801, whose egalitarianism, evangelical Protestantism, and promotion of black churches reinforced the inherent desire on the part of Negroes for freedom.

As restiveness among slaves increased toward the end of the eighteenth century, Bertie became a center of alarm. In 1798 authorities arrested three slaves in the county who were suspected of heading a conspiracy of 150 men armed with guns, swords, and knives. Accused of attacking patrollers, the three leaders were convicted of contravening "the laws and dignity of the state" and punished with thirty-nine lashes and cropped ears.

By 1802 rumors of a more general slave insurrection panicked North Carolinians. Reaching into Virginia and influenced by the Gabriel Prosser revolt in Richmond in 1800, the plot in North Carolina was to climax in June with a massive uprising. Bertie County patrollers uncovered the scheme in early June when they discovered a note containing the names of reputed rebels in one of the Negro houses of Colerain. The suspects were quickly apprehended and eight days later tried by the county court. Six conspirators were hanged immediately, including Bob, a slave belonging to Senator David Stone, one of the members of the court. Altogether, the court executed eleven slaves, deported another six, and whipped and cropped the ears of twenty more. The conspiracy kept eastern North Carolina in turmoil during the summer months of 1802, though the whites, as always, mounted a concerted counterattack and effectively maintained their authority in the face of the defiant slaves.

Although the next serious slave scare occurred in 1831 as a result of the Nat Turner insurrection in Virginia, Bertie continued to experience rebelliousness among its black population. On a spring day in 1810 James Hayes informed Anthony Wiggins, his mulatto servant and overseer, that the slaves had accomplished too little and demanded more effort from the bondsmen. Wiggins replied that the slaves could not and should not be expected to work harder, whereupon Hayes hit him with a root of a tree. Wiggins retaliated by striking his master with a hoe, killing him with several blows. The slaves did nothing to prevent the murder; instead they helped Wiggins conceal the body.

The Nat Turner insurrection, the South's bloodiest slave revolt, occurred in Southampton County, Virginia, in August, 1831. In Bertie, geographically removed from the scene of the uprising only by Northampton and Hertford counties, the fears and tensions that always lurked below the surface of antebellum society were revealed by the arming of its white citizens, the reinforcement of the patrol system, and the undue suspicion of slave activity. Yet, despite Bertie's proximity to Virginia and

11

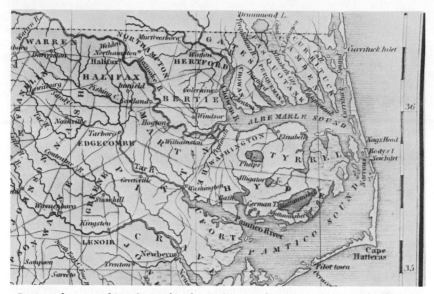

Portion of a map of North Carolina by Anthony Finley in *A New General Atlas, 1824* (Philadelphia, 1824), p. 19.

the fact that the majority of the county's inhabitants were slaves, neither the *Edenton Gazette*, the *Raleigh Register*, nor private correspondence reported the hysteria and confusion in Bertie that characterized so many areas of the state, including New Hanover County far to the south.

The Nat Turner insurrection did nothing to abate the practice of slavery. On the contrary it made whites more defensive of their institution and more determined to subject properly their bonded property. The "peculiar institution" not only thrived but underwent a process of concentration in Bertie. The number of slaveholders in the county stabilized—469 in 1840 as opposed to 468 in 1860—but the number of slaves increased, reaching 8,185 in the latter year, and average slaveholdings rose from 14.3 to 17.5. Two of the fifteen planters in North Carolina who possessed at least 200 slaves resided in Bertie.

In addition to arousing white fears of slave insurrection, Nat Turner reinforced suspicions of free Negroes who were perceived as a dangerous, "incendiary" element of society. The 1830-1831 legislature, alarmed by the publication of black abolitionist David Walker's *Appeal* in 1829, had already passed a number of punitive statutes, called collectively the "Free Negro Code" by historian John Hope Franklin, which were designed to circumscribe the liberties of free blacks. The Constitutional

Convention of 1835 added to the ignominy of the code by depriving free Negroes of the suffrage. Toward the approach of the Civil War the state legislature considered banishing free Negroes from North Carolina or perhaps enslaving those who remained. After more than twenty left Tarboro in nearby Edgecombe County in early 1861, the *Tarboro Mercury* commented, "The riddance is a good one, and we hope that others of the same class will follow this excellent example." Sentiment among whites in Bertie doubtlessly differed little.

Actually free Negroes in Bertie always remained few in number. Although only Northampton and Halifax counted more in 1790, the 348 free Negroes in Bertie constituted 2.8 percent of the county's population. Slightly less than half were clustered in twenty-six households; the remainder were scattered among white families, probably as apprentices. By 1860 the number had dwindled to 319 or 2.2 percent of the county's inhabitants. At that time twenty-nine counties exceeded Bertie in their number of free Negroes.

Economically, free Negroes fared poorly. In 1830 four black women and one black man reported the ownership of a total of eleven slaves; five black farmers owned their land. By 1860 free Negro slave owners had disappeared, and only twenty-nine free Negroes in Bertie owned any real or personal property. Its total value amounted to one half of 1 percent of the aggregate value of property possessed by free Negroes in the state. Not numbers or property but status—free people of color who not only posed a threat to the color line but who also were potentially dangerous as persons most likely to create disturbing passions among the slaves—brought forth the wrath of whites against free Negroes.

After the Civil War the 1870 census showed a 9-percent drop in the Bertie population over the past decade, primarily the result of the exodus of former slaves. Blacks truly found the war a liberating experience. Those who did not escape to freedom behind Federal lines served the Union army in various ways, including that of informant. As one white in Bertie said in 1864, he could do nothing that would violate orders from the occupying army, for the "negroes will tell them everything."

Following 1870 the population of the county rose slowly but steadily until it peaked at 26,439 in 1950. Advances in medical science and public health lowered mortality rates and increased longevity. Although Negroes from North Carolina's Second Congressional District, the "Black Second" of which Bertie was a part, left the state in large numbers in the 1870s and 1880s, blacks in Bertie continued to increase. By 1920 Bertie's ratio of Negro to white inhabitants was the seventh highest in the state, as blacks continued to average 56 to 60 percent of the county's population.

After 1950 Bertie's population began a precipitate contraction, dipping to 20,528 by 1970 as poverty and bleak employment opportunities haunted the county and forced an outmigration that was more pronounced among Negroes than whites. From 1960 to 1970 the number of blacks in Bertie declined by almost 20 percent, double the figure for whites. According to the Reverend Andrew J. Cherry, "New York was the haven for most of the people of Bertie County." During the 1970s, however, the emigration trend was halted. Preliminary census counts for 1980 show that Bertie's population rose to 21,024, an increase of 2.4 percent.

WEALTH, HEALTH,
AND ENTERTAINMENT

Although North Carolina has been accounted a land of small farmers and, sometimes contemptuously, a wellspring of democracy in its early years, the concept of class distinction characterized colonial society. Bertie was no exception. The upper class or gentry, distinguished by superior wealth, education, and worldly pretension, provided political as well as cultural leadership. The middle and lower orders constituted the most numerous segments of the population. Their life-styles revealed minimal resources and unpolished breeding. Although often kind, hospitable, and generous, they were also rude, noisy, and uncouth.

Indentured servants and free Negroes followed the three principal classes on the social scale. Servants, crucially important in peopling the southern colonies, were well represented in Bertie. Tax lists for 1763 and 1768 show that they made up one fourth to one third of the free taxable population of the county. The servants appeared in a quarter of the Bertie households, though more than 70 percent of those families registered only one taxable servant and none had more than four. After the Revolution the institution of indentured servitude dwindled in significance as slavery assumed paramountcy in the nonfree labor market.

Revealing the alarmingly inequitable distribution of wealth in colonial Bertie is the investigation of historians Marvin L. M. Kay and Lorin L. Cary, who have found that in the years just prior to the Revolution the lower 30 percent of the free population in Bertie owned 1.7 percent of the wealth, the middle 30 percent, 7.9 percent of the wealth, the upper 30 percent, 31.6 percent of the wealth, and the upper 10 percent, 58.8 percent of the wealth. Money, of course, meant political power, and the leading county officials evidenced a greater concentration of wealth than that found among the richest 10 percent of the county's inhabitants. While the average inventoried wealth in Bertie was £435.10.0 and £2,560 for the wealthiest 10 percent of the populace, county officials averaged £2,854.

One of those county officials was John Campbell, a self-made merchant-planter called by Governor Arthur Dobbs in 1760, "the most eminent Trader in this Province." Campbell owned thousands of acres of land in Bertie, Chowan, Hertford, and other eastern counties plus 12,500 acres in Anson County. At his death in 1781 he owned thirty-six slaves, the usual complement of livestock, and over $4,250 in various continental and state currencies. In his house were 8 feather beds, a beaufet (buffet), numerous tables, cupboards, 41 chairs, 44 pictures, a dumbwaiter, an ivory-headed cane, a clock, and a "Speaking Trumpet." Three card tables, two backgammon tables, and a cribbage table indicated his preference for gaming. Campbell's library contained 358 books in English, Latin, and French as well as pamphlets, magazines, sermons, laws, and newspapers. In addition, an unknown number of books had been loaned to others. Among other myriad possessions were two carts and two riding chairs, the latter a sure badge of superior wealth and status at the time.

In the antebellum era wealth continued to concentrate in the hands of the few. According to the 1860 census there were twenty-five plantations in Bertie containing a thousand or more acres, a figure unsurpassed by any other county. Actually, only four other counties boasted as many as ten plantations of that acreage. Slave ownership was likewise skewed. Only Edgecombe and Warren counties had more than the thirty-five slaveholders in Bertie who claimed at least fifty bondsmen.

Representing the elite of the pre-Civil War years was John B. Williams, whose lavish manner of living must have evoked envy in most social circles. In the early 1840s Williams dressed in "fine" satin vests, a black Italian cravat, silk and cashmere hose, and various articles of clothing made from Manchester gingham and blue alpaca. The adjective "best" often described his purchases, whether clothes, brandy, or playing cards. Williams could afford to remain away from home for months at a time, incurring such expenses as boarding two horses for $20 a month. He spent much time in Norfolk where he patronized the firm of Paul & Pegram, "Dealers in Staple and Fancy Dry Goods." Williams also regaled in the smoke of fine "Regalia" cigars, purchasing as many as five dozen a month.

Probably the best survey of elite antebellum life in Bertie is found in *Bertie: Or, Life in the Old Field. A Humorous Novel*, written by George H. Throop under the pseudonym of Gregory Seaworthy and published by a Philadelphia firm in 1851. Together with the same author's *Nags Head: Or, Two Months among "The Bankers,"* which emerged from press the previous year, *Bertie* provided North Carolina with its first contemporary fictional treatment by one who wrote of the life he knew and of which he had been a part. According to the author, a tutor for the Capehart family at Scotch Hall, life was never dull for the families living along the Chowan River, the principal setting of *Bertie*. They visited and dined with one another, fished and hunted, and enjoyed the excitement of "mail days" at the nearest post office. The Christmas season was especially festive, even for the Negroes who reveled in the John Kooner tradition of drinking, dancing, and holiday merrymaking, while in the summer schooners loaded with furniture and livestock took the wealthy to Nags Head for two or three months.

16

George Higby Throop (1818-1896), a native of New York, wrote two novels based on his experience as a tutor to the children of the Capehart family in Bertie County. Under the pseudonym of Gregory Seaworthy he published *Nags Head* in 1850 and *Bertie* in 1851.

Scotch Hall was the setting for Throop's novels on antebellum plantation life; he spent about seven months there in 1849. George Washington Capehart (d. 1885) built Scotch Hall in 1838. It was the center of the largest plantation complex in Bertie County, consisting of 8,000 acres worked by nearly 300 slaves.

In contrast to Campbell, Williams, and the rich who congregated along the rivers in their imposing estates were the less fortunate like Hezekiah Callum, whose entire fortune in 1793 consisted of his "Waring aperal," a hat, two pairs of shoes, a pair of shoe buckles, a pair of knee buckles, a bedstead, some leather and crockery, and a horse, saddle, and bridle. The petitions of Bertie Revolutionary War veterans for government support likewise reveal poverty-stricken conditions in the county. In 1820 Ezekiel White, a sixty-five-year-old farmer, submitted a property schedule that consisted of eighty-four acres of land, an eleven-year-old horse, two cows, two hogs, a chest and table, and two "old" spinning wheels. Another veteran, James Outlaw, sixty years old and greatly afflicted with rheumatism, claimed three plows, two axes, a linen wheel, a bed, and some plates, knives, and forks, all of which served to maintain a family of six.

Just as there were extremes in wealth among men, so did worldly riches vary greatly among the women. Catherine Hunter, an orphan possessing a substantial estate, almost casually purchased "fine" cardinals, riding hats with gold buttons and loops, satin bonnets, silk hose, silver shoe buckles, necklaces, and yards of the best cloth during her wardship from 1772 to 1775. At her death in 1791 Olive Carter owned a feather bed, two spinning wheels, dishes, plates, bottles, and a basin. Her wardrobe included a scarlet cloak, a cotton cloak, a linen jacket, five gowns, five petticoats, three linen shifts, several aprons, handkerchiefs, a pair of gloves, and a pair of shoes. Jewelry consisted of silver buckles, silver buttons, three gold rings, and two bracelets. A fan, snuffbox, spun and unspun cotton, and "a handkerchief full of sundries" completed her inventory.

In contrast, when Sarah Cherry died in 1806, her estate comprised a desk, dish, pot, pair of steelyards, a small trunk, and "Some waring cloths." Thomas B. Hardy, administrator of the estate of Elizabeth Powell, reported the sale of her property as $157.70 in 1855. That sum, $5.50 in cash found in a trunk, the receipt of an additional $6.00, and interest raised the total value of her estate to $174.11, but $83.16 in expenses left a balance of only $90.95. Still, that was greater than the net worth of Elizabeth Jenkins's estate, which in the same year amounted to $44.73. In 1860, when the widow of Henry Casper petitioned the county court for a year's provisions from her deceased husband's estate, she received 10 pounds of corn, 300 pounds of salt pork, 25 pounds of coffee, 50 pounds of sugar, 10 gallons of molasses, 100 pounds of flour, 75 pounds of lard, and some Irish potatoes and peas.

The homes of the people, like their personal possessions, manifested class distinction. The elite in some instances erected fine brick structures accompanied by the usual outbuildings. Exemplifying the use of brick in Bertie was Joseph A. Brown, who in 1807 described his plantation house on the Chowan River as "a large comfortable brick Dwelling House, with 6 rooms on the first floor, surrounded with piazzas, situated 200 yards from the river, [with] a court yard surrounded with handsome railed fencing, near two acres of garden, also enclosed by paling, a two story Kitchen, brick store House, large Barn Stable, Corn Cribs, &c. &c."

Brick was rare, however, and even among the wealthy wood was the primary construction material. Hope Plantation, built by Governor David Stone about 1810 and restored in the late 1960s, is a magnificent country house and an outstanding example of a Federal period residence reflecting Jeffersonian classicism with its Palladian influence. As was common among the wealthy, Stone adapted the plan of his home from an English architectural manual, in his case Abraham Swan's *The British Architect.*

The less fortunate satisfied themselves with more modest frame or clapboard houses, and many continued to live in log cabins, which remained a prominent construction style even after the turn of the nineteenth century. Most of the houses were small, poorly ventilated, and simply constructed. Dr. Jeremiah Battle's observation about Edgecombe County in 1810—"the style of building in Tarboro is as it is in the country, generally plain and cheap"—undoubtedly applied to Bertie. In sum, the often used term, "tolerable dwelling," best characterized most homes.

Other aspects of life, the treatment of illness, for example, reflected socioeconomic status. The high cost (and sometimes dubious results) of professional medical treatment compelled many to resort to home remedies and treatises like *Everyman His Own Doctor* (1734). Only the fortunate availed themselves of the care of a physician. The family (including slaves) of Stark B. Smith necessitated visits and medication from Charles B. Skiles on nineteen of the thirty days in June, 1857, accumulating a bill of $45.00 for the month and charges of $214.12 for the year. And one had to pick his personal physician carefully. In the 1750s Dr. Robert Lenox, who obtained his degree from Edinburgh and was one of the very few university-trained physicians in North Carolina at the time, treated the family of John Campbell. In one of the most scandalous malpractice cases in the early history of North Carolina Dr. Lenox, during the course of his ministrations to the family, attempted to seduce Campbell's wife, reportedly gaining her confidence by means of an aphrodisiac. The two unsuccessfully tried to poison Campbell and on another occasion attempted to elope to the West Indies before they were discovered.

Whether competent or deceitful, physicians offered treatment that varied little from the eighteenth to the first half of the nineteenth century. Medicines ordered by Cullen Pollock from N. Gregory in Norfolk in 1819—paregoric, Peruvian bark, rattlesnake root, ipecac, rhubarb, calomel, opium, blistering salve—had been used for many years and would be popular for decades to come. Illustrative of the medical ministrations were the accounts of Dr. James Jones in 1824, which included charges principally for febrifuge mixtures, blister plasters, Peruvian bark, opium pills, borax of soda, emetics, and cathartics.

Neither professional help nor home concoctions could combat effectively the baneful malaria that was so prevalent in Bertie or the many other diseases that beset residents of the county. The mortality schedule for Bertie for the year ending June 1, 1850, shows that 135 people or 1 percent of the population died. Most succumbed to various forms of respiratory illnesses. Pneumonia accounted for 14 percent of the known causes of death. Pleurisy, bilious pleurisy, consumption, colic, and croup carried off another 20 percent. Fevers, whether bilious, congestive, or typhoid, resulted in 13 percent of the deaths, and "inflammation of the bowels," the single greatest killer other than pneumonia, also accounted for 13 percent of the deaths. Accidents—a drowning, two deaths by lightning, and one killed by a falling tree—claimed another four lives. Other deaths resulted from dropsy, old age, childbirth, scrofula, and worms.

Further analysis of the mortality statistics reveals a preponderance of Negroes and children among the deceased. Although blacks constituted only 58.5 percent of the population, they accounted for 65 percent of those who died in 1850. The mortality rate for children was alarmingly high. One fifth of those who died had not reached one year of age; another 24 percent were less than five years old upon their deaths. Clearly, if one passed infancy and early childhood, his chances of survival were excellent, though there was no assurance that he would approach the age of the slave Fortune, 112, when she died.

Additional insight into the nature of mortality derives from the county coroner's investigations of accidental and violent deaths. Of the twenty-eight surviving inquests for the 1840s one fourth involved murders, including that of a white woman beaten to death with a sharp-edged tool and left in a swamp. Accidents took their toll also. Six persons drowned in the waters of the county, five burned to death when their clothing caught fire, and two young children froze on a January night in 1848 when they "wandered off unknown to their parents."

Those who enjoyed the advantage of some longevity availed themselves of the traditional amusements and entertainments of agrarian society in early North Carolina. Teas, visitations, and quilting bees occupied the ladies. Dancing was immensely popular with both sexes. Men appreciated wrestling and boxing matches, long bullets, bandy, and bowls. At the taverns they gathered for cards, backgammon, shuffleboard, and billiards. In 1724, after the construction of the first courthouse for the county, the Bertie justices of the peace granted William Daniel's petition to build a tavern on the courthouse lot due to the "great want of Publick houses to entertain the People" who attended court.

Among the favorite pastimes of the men were horse racing, cockfighting, fishing, and hunting. In 1731 Edmond Wiggons accused William Jones of stealing a £5 bill while they watched a horse race at the house of John Taylor. Serving to provide food, eliminate predatory animals, while away the hours, and satisfy the sporting instinct, hunting sometimes assumed the guise of public entertainment. In November, 1836, a grand squirrel hunt originated in Windsor. Twenty men were selected for contending parties with the understanding that those who returned with the least game would provide a hot meal for the victors. When the hunt was completed, the winning party had killed 9,814 squirrels; the losers, only 7,543.

Also commanding the attention of large numbers of people were the public celebrations. For recognizing the Fourth of July in 1812, "an elegant and sumptuous dinner" was prepared for those in Windsor who gathered on the green in front of the courthouse about two o'clock. After drinking to seventeen prepared and three volunteer toasts, the crowd ate, watched the firing of cannon, and sang patriotic songs. Another lavish celebration marked the Fourth in 1838 when a public dinner in Wilkinson's Tavern was accompanied by the usual toasts and orations. Unfortunately, three or four "drunken fellows" marred the proceedings by smashing bottles. In the evening the Windsor Thespians offered a production, two "medical" gentlemen discharged fireworks, and a cannon boomed to conclude the festivities.

Crowds also gathered for the touring theatrical companies that visited the county. In August, 1838, the Windsor Thespians graciously received a group consisting of a woman and her two daughters and two sons. In order to avoid the county tax on theatrical productions, the company agreed not to charge for its performance, though all understood that they would donate a gratuity equal to the usual admission fee. According to William D. Valentine, the company "acquitted themselves well." However, the gossipy Valentine could not help but add the observation that the woman had been accused six years earlier in Philadelphia of murdering her husband. Though found innocent of the charge and released, she perhaps found traveling expedient.

In his diary Valentine also commented caustically upon another diversion in 1838. His entry for May 10 noted that the "all engrossing amusement" of Windsor was the "dirty fingered game" of marbles. Wrote Valentine, "The young men appear run mad with this child's play and wine and porter pay the winners," at least when the youth were not engaged in "Fornication and adultery and letchery," which were "boldly practiced . . . without fear or shame." Marbles, if not immorality, continued to be popular. John B. Williams purchased fifteen in 1842, perhaps for his child, and in the early years of the twentieth century Aulander commissioners imposed fines on marble players who obstructed traffic in the town.

On the eve of the Civil War tax returns for Bertie revealed a thoroughly rural, moderately prosperous county that ranked between the acknowledged riches of neighboring Edgecombe and the relative poverty of Nash County. In 1855 the valuation of town property in Bertie was $39,345 compared to $58,928 in Edgecombe and $9,000 in Nash. Other than town property, land in Bertie was valued at $3.66 per acre as opposed to $4.47 in Edgecombe and $1.98 in Nash. Comparisons of personalty are similarly instructive. Bertie citizens paid taxes of $107 on gold watches, $42 on pianos, and $172 on pleasure carriages. Figures for the respective returns in Edgecombe were $175, $59, and $446; in Nash, $77, $30, and $227.

The war, of course, gravely disrupted Bertie life. Prosperous planter S. A. Norfleet, who had married in 1860, spending $115 for the bridal present and $1,067.50 for the wedding trip to northern spas, turned from the remunerative cultivation of cotton to the less profitable production of wheat and oats during the conflict. Federal troops periodically raided the county, killing George Capehart's cattle and chasing his hogs so that the animals became "very wild." Significant shortages of necessary items appeared. Capehart's overseer, writing in 1864 to his employer who had taken refuge in Franklin County, reported that paper was unavailable for purchase and that he was able to write only because a friendly Union soldier had given him a sheet.

After the war Bertie, like the rest of the South, suffered from poverty and destruction. However, there were exceptions, represented by Elizabeth Outlaw. From April to December, 1866, Miss Outlaw purchased from a local store two pairs of shoes, a scarlet cloak, a linen cloak, a Shaker bonnet, a corset, and various clothing materials, including linen, calico, cotton, jeans, shirting, silk, burlap, and ruffling along with pins, needles, and buttons. She also acquired two quires of paper, a pack of envelopes, two fans, and two fine combs. While others faced deprivation, Miss Outlaw dressed well and lived lavishly.

The war only briefly interrupted the busy social schedule of Miss Sallie Smith of Woodville. In 1866 her social calendar included a picnic at Palmyra in May and "grand tournaments and balls" at Enfield in June, at Jones Spring in July, and at Halifax in September. Her surviving invitations indicate the probable attendance of dances in Scotland Neck and Halifax in 1868 and again in Scotland Neck the next year. Also in 1869 Miss Smith received invitations to a dance at the home of Mr. P. E. Smith and to a ball and party at Plymouth. In the 1870s she continued on the social circuit to enjoy a "Fancy and Dress Ball" at the state agricultural fair and a picnic at Tuscarora Mineral Springs.

The elite also continued to patronize Nags Head, take steamer excursions along the Chowan River, attend magnificent dances, enjoy sumptuous meals, and delight in spas. Examples of private entertainment in the 1890s included the Klondike Party at Colerain for the benefit of the Colerain Methodist Church, the "Masked feast" or "festival incognito" at the American House Hotel in Windsor, and the "Literary Charade" offered the young people of Colerain by Dr. and Mrs. Newell, at which there were prizes for naming the most books, dinner, dancing, and a fireworks display. The names of Francis D. Winston, the eminent politician, and his wife were often found in the social columns of the *Windsor Ledger* as hosts for various gatherings such as a Chinese Tea in December, 1896.

Traveling shows, circuses, and fairs provided more general public entertainment. The Jolly Fun Makers, an "excellent company of clever and well-behaved actors and actresses," offered a satire on the Spanish-American War and other comedies for the people of Windsor in 1899. The following year the Sun Brothers Circus gave the usual street parade and then the big show featuring a trained animal exhibition. For those

23

who missed the circus in Windsor, a county fair and carnival were held at Lewiston the next month, sponsored by the Southern Carnival Association and the Industrial Department of the Seaboard Air Line Railroad. All were invited to bring any exhibit from "the coarsest farm product to the finest needle work."

Two of the most popular forms of recreation to emerge in the last years of the nineteenth century were baseball and cycling. Many of the Bertie communities organized baseball teams, though in 1897 the *Windsor Ledger* boasted that the Windsor club would be one of the most powerful in the state. Its strength lay in its manager, Captain William Hindley, Jr., who was not only "a gentleman well up in base-ball management, but handsome, genial and a clever player." Indeed, at a celebration of the annual reunion of Confederate veterans in the summer of 1897, the Windsor club defeated a select team from the rest of the county.

Baseball at least shared the recreational spotlight with cycling, a sport that appealed to ladies as well as men. At the veterans reunion there was also a bicycle parade and numerous races with prizes awarded to the owner of "the most appropriate decorated machine" and the winners of the races. The Windsor Town Cyclers organized by the following year and proceeded to lay off a track and give exhibitions of their riding skills. They offered their first bicycle meet and field day exercise in September, 1898. By 1900 tax figures for the county reported 144 bicycles valued at $1,830.

Health care improved after the war, though competent physicians remained relatively few and centered in Windsor. Perforce, many continued to depend upon home remedies and resort to across-the-counter or mail-order medicines. Beecham's Pills, advertised in 1895, appealed to those with ailments that ranged from biliousness and foul breath to sallow skin and torpid liver. Scott's Emulsion rectified consumption, scrofula, and loss of flesh, at the same time helping thin babies, weak children, and "all conditions of Wasting." Such medicines, along with "Quackery with a bolder front than ever known heretofore in the history of our profession," prompted Drs. Edward W. Pugh, Luther A. Newell, and Wayland Mitchell in 1897 to call for the organization of a county medical society to curb the "itinerant hawkers of spectacles," the crossroads grocery that usurped the function of the pharmacist, and all other "grades and classes of quacksalvers, charlatans, and mountebanks."

Certainly the people were unprepared for the mild smallpox epidemic that threatened the county in 1899. Although Jenner's momentous discovery of cowpox inoculation to combat smallpox was a century old, many North Carolinians had not been vaccinated. However, the county commissioners acted quickly to demand the isolation and vaccination of those who came in contact with the disease as well as the vaccination of schoolchildren. Some opposition arose to the latter proposition, evoking the opinion of the attorney general of the state that the commissioners had acted within their authority in ordering the vaccination of the children.

As the county realized progress in the field of medicine, reform also touched people in such areas as temperance. William D. Valentine noted in 1838 that people tried to disguise themselves by "Blacking and painting their faces" as they were "Staggering and swaggering about the streets" of Windsor but to little avail. By 1874 the *Albemarle Times* was editorializing on the "ills and evils of whiskey drinking," though in a statewide referendum on prohibition a decade later less than 10 percent of the Bertie voters supported the reform. Yet by 1897 the "drys" in the county convinced the county commissioners to cease granting liquor licenses and another referendum in 1908 produced an affirmative vote for prohibition.

Although the experiment in prohibition ultimately failed, the quality of life in Bertie improved in the twentieth century. Better transportation, particularly via the automobile, and communication opened new vistas for travel and recreation. Dances or "germans" continued to be popular, "Old Soldiers Day" remained a festive occasion, motion pictures became a popular entertainment medium, and boating supplemented hunting and fishing as a recreational pastime. Numerous civic, social, patriotic, and charitable organizations either appeared or continued their activities including the Masons, whose Charity Lodge No. 5 succeeded in 1822 the Royal Edwin Lodge, one of the oldest lodges in the state.

Despite the good fortunes of Miss Capehart, Miss Smith, and others, the Civil War had a devastating effect on the Bertie economy. While it freed the majority of the county's inhabitants who had been held in bondage, those people were bereft of property, education, and prospects of finding meaningful employment. Thus in 1850 the county had cared for twenty-five paupers. In 1870 the number rose sixfold to 150 (93 whites and 57 Negroes), necessitating an outlay of $3,500. From August, 1873, to August, 1874, the county provided monetary assistance to 187 persons in amounts that varied from $2.50 to $00.00. The county also maintained a Home for the Aged and Infirm, which by the 1890s additionally housed prisoners or convicts.

Impoverished county residents did not go unnoticed in the twentieth century. A survey of government services in the 1920s showed that Bertie continued to maintain a "farm" (actually two, but one was unused) about four miles from Windsor on the Cashie River for the aged, infirm, poor, and criminals. An average of thirty persons annually were housed on the farm at a monthly cost of $3.31 per person. Whites were boarded in cottages sufficiently large for two or three persons; blacks in one large dwelling. Two of the Negro men were eligible for Civil War pensions, one for service in the Confederacy, the other for service in the United States government. However, they enjoyed life on the county farm and received better care than their meager stipends would otherwise have allowed. Since Windsor did not maintain a jail, prisoners awaiting or serving sentence went to the farm where they constituted the principal source of labor for cultivating the approximately 200 acres of cleared land on which were raised vegetables, peanuts, cotton, and corn.

In addition to supporting the county farm Bertie employed a health officer, though his manifold duties that ranged from licensing cooks in public restaurants to training midwives rendered his overall efforts less than satisfactory. There was no single welfare officer in the county. Instead, those responsibilities were assumed by the county commissioners and the superintendent of schools. Nevertheless, one observer declared that the most knowledgeable person in the county in the area of welfare services was Mrs. Francis D. Winston. She exercised considerable influence in the decisions of the commissioners when they conceived programs and disbursed moneys. On the whole, little planning or coordination of social services existed, an understandable situation when the people of the county begrudged "every dollar spent in [welfare] work. . . ."

Fifty years later the need for social services funding had by no means diminished, for Bertie by most statistics was one of North Carolina's poorest counties. The unemployment rate for Bertie averaged 30 percent higher than that for the state in the decade of the seventies. The lack of modern plumbing facilities in over 40 percent of the homes in Bertie in 1977 far exceeded the average for North Carolina. In 1970 median family income averaged $4,829 in the county as opposed to $7,774 in the state, and the 37.5 percent of the families with incomes below the poverty level was one of the highest figures for any county in North Carolina. Negro families fared worst—over one half realized less than poverty level incomes.

Progress has been made, however, though Bertie's prospects are not altogether auspicious. Modern housing underwritten by the Federal Housing Authority has replaced many sharecropper homes in the 1970s. Other federal programs have also helped to mitigate poverty-stricken conditions. The county health department and the Bertie County Memorial Hospital located in Windsor offer modern medical facilities to county residents. Yet Bertie remains troubled by problems that characterize many rural areas of the state and nation. The county lacks sufficient industry to expand its tax base and generate employment, its educational system depends substantially upon outside support, and the county loses bright young people to better job prospects beyond its borders, a circumstance noted by the *Windsor Ledger* in 1900 when it commented, "Many young men of Bertie county are constantly leaving here seeking their livelihood or fortune. . . ." Finally, through no fault of its own, Bertie remains rather isolated, cut off from major cities, ports, and transportation facilities such as airports and interstate highways that might serve to stimulate economic expansion and improve the general standard of living.

EDUCATION

In the eighteenth century educational opportunities for the scattered, relatively poor, agrarian populace of North Carolina proved limited. Colonial governors, English clergymen, and travelers often commented on the benighted colonials of the province. During the Revolution Elkanah Watson wrote, "Perhaps no State had at that period performed so little to promote the cause of education, science and arts, as North Carolina. The lower classes . . . were . . . in a condition of great mental degradation." Historians have rarely been more charitable. According to Louis B. Wright, "North Carolina was the most backward of the colonies in matters of education. . . ."

Though somewhat atypical of North Carolina counties by virtue of its proximity to water and world trade as well as to the cultural influence of Virginia, Bertie probably contained only a small percentage of functionally literate inhabitants. Those fortunate enough to secure the rudiments of the three Rs obtained their instruction from teachers in the old field schools, tutors, siblings, and parents. In a 1788 deposition Henry Abbot claimed that he had kept a "school in the uper eand of Bertie County near Norflets ferry" about twenty-four years ago "or upwards." In the early 1770s Billy Dawson, son of John and Penelope Dawson, secured his initial instruction in a "neighborhood school." After the departure of the schoolmaster, Billy's mother supervised his education and directed his "reading four times a day & writing twice"; she believed that "he was never kept half so strict with any of his masters."

Education involved more than formal instruction, however. Young men and women also prepared to assume their proper stations in life. Reflecting the hierarchical nature of society, legislation in 1715 directed that orphans with sufficient estates be placed with guardians who would educate and provide for the children "according to their Rank & degree." Otherwise the orphans were to be apprenticed to learn a handicraft or trade. Poor, orphan girls, like Marendo Goff in 1759, learned "Sewing & Household Business." Indigent boys were apprenticed most often to coopers, shoemakers, and blacksmiths, though many found homes with carpenters, tailors, bricklayers, weavers, hatters, merchants, mariners, and farmers in order to acquire the skills of those occupations.

For the upper strata of society young gentlemen required considerably more learning, formal as well as practical, and hoped also to attain some proficiency in playing a musical instrument and dancing. For young ladies of consequence Governor Gabriel Johnston's will of 1751 exemplified the hopes of an aristocratic father when he stipulated that his daughter be brought up "in the Fear of God, in Sobriety and Moderation [,] Confining her desires to things Plain, neat and Elegant, and Especially . . . to keep within the Bounds of her Income. . . ." That young girl became Mrs. Penelope Dawson, who was later described by James Iredell as "generally allowed to be above all kind of competition" in her "excellence of understanding, Goodness of heart, and . . . most polite, attractive behaviour."

Educational facilities improved in the nineteenth century as witnessed by the opening of such schools as that sponsored by Drew Whitmill at New-Market in 1810. Whitmill advertised the instructor, Henry W. Rhodes, as a young man of "liberal education" who had taught in Hertford County during the previous year, and who would offer instruction in Latin, geography, English grammar, and arithmetic. Whitmill announced that he would accept ten to twelve scholars as boarders and that parents could rest assured "that the utmost attention will be paid to their morals." Such an advantageous opportunity, he hoped, would induce at least "the gentlemen" of the county to patronize the school.

Beyond the schools' offering the fundamentals of education were the academies, finishing schools for most and springboards to college for some. The academy movement began in earnest in North Carolina after the Revolution. By the Civil War almost 300 such institutions had been chartered by the state legislature with varying degrees of success. Several opened in Bertie, including Bertie Union Academy, which advertised in the *Raleigh Register* its semiannual examinations for June, 1825. John D. Tate, the only teacher at the school, which was characterized as "being in its infancy," taught spelling, grammar, reading, and arithmetic in addition to Latin and Greek. Eight years later Oak Grove Academy in Bertie advertised its semiannual student exercises. By 1850 the county claimed five private schools, three for males, two for females. Together they enrolled 110 students.

Those parents or guardians who sought educational advantages for their children beyond the county could avail themselves of numerous academies and finishing schools in the state as well as the University of North Carolina. Molly and James C. Cherry, wards of David Outlaw, completed their education at the Chowan Female Collegiate Institute in Murfreesboro and the University of North Carolina at Chapel Hill respectively. Molly attended the institute from 1856 to 1859, studying English, history, rhetoric, botany, and philosophy while taking piano lessons and acquiring a proficiency in painting. Her brother James was enrolled at the university at the same time. According to his purchases at the bookstore, he was reading Horace, calculating logarithms, and enjoying such novels as *Lost Daughter, Banished Love,* and *Love Me Little, Love Me Long.*

29

Those who left home remained close in the minds of their families if Susan B. Capehart and her son William were representative. Sent to an Edenton school in the mid-1840s, William received the constant attention of his mother as well as letters from his father and grandfather despite the nearness of his home, Scotch Hall plantation. Susan Capehart "repaired" William's shirts, darned socks, and sent among other items apples, oranges, sponge cake, butter, and nuts, the last of which made William ill. She also worried about the baneful influence of town life in Edenton, directing William not to "stay about stores and shops for you can gain nothing good by doing so. . . . [Too] many persons loiter about such places . . . [and] I do not think it proper for little boys to hear every thing men chat about."

The Civil War only briefly interrupted the educational routine of Bertie. By 1870 nine private schools offering instruction to 127 pupils served the county. In addition there were two classical academies. One enrolled ten male students; the other, fifteen young ladies.

The Windsor High School, catering to boys and girls, thrived in the 1870s. Its principal, Joseph J. Freeman, advertised in 1876 that the institution prepared "students for College, or for the practical duties of life. A watchful parental discipline will aim at the moral as well as intellectual elevation of the pupil." By the 1890s the high school had given way to the Windsor Academy. According to the *Windsor Ledger*, a male student could ready himself to enter the state university or any college in the nation and a young lady could gain admission to Greensboro after graduation by the academy. Among its curriculum were courses in business, telegraphy, and shorthand as well as pedagogy, which was particularly "designed for the better preparation of public and private school teachers."

In 1890 the town of Windsor also housed the Rosefield Institute for young ladies, Miss Minnie Gray's school for boys and girls, a private school directed by Miss L. O. Williams, and the Rankin-Richards Institute. Mrs. Mary F. Gillam and her daughter Helen managed the Rosefield Institute, which provided students with instruction in Latin, German, French, higher mathematics, elocution, and music in addition to the "common school course." By 1900 Miss Gray, who enjoyed an excellent reputation as a teacher in the county, had abandoned her school to become an assistant principal at the Windsor Academy. The Rankin-Richards Institute, designed for black children and operated by Rhoden Mitchell, enrolled 154 boys and girls in 1890. It became the Bertie Academy in 1901.

Elsewhere in the county several private schools and academies, including Roxobel Academy, Aulander Academy, Colerain School, Cashie

Preparatory at Cashie Neck, and Woodville School, offered tutelage to the youth of Bertie. Altogether the academies and schools enrolled 323 students in 1890, though the number fluctuated greatly. For example, in 1899 the Aulander Academy counted 143 boys and girls, a fourfold increase over the total of 35 at the beginning of the decade.

Despite the existence of the several private institutions of learning in the county, in the latter half of the nineteenth century the public school system became the principal means of educating Bertie children. In 1839 the North Carolina legislature enacted its first statute to support a public school system. William W. Cherry, Whig senator from Bertie, introduced the bill in the upper house. By 1850 Bertie had thirty-two common schools that enrolled over a thousand students. The Civil War disrupted the public school system, however, and in 1870 only 165 boys and 171 girls attended public schools in the county.

Still, one of the most laudable achievements of the Republicans during Reconstruction was the creation of a biracial and enduring public school system. During the so-called "Fusion" period, 1895-1901, when Populists and Republicans briefly wrested control from the Democrats, blacks sometimes dominated the county school board. The *Windsor Ledger* often castigated black educational leadership, but the paper staunchly supported the principle of public education for both races, only demanding white domination of the decision-making apparatus and the segregation of school facilities. And, indeed, after 1898, that was the foundation of public education in the county for over a half century.

During the 1890s R. W. Askew, perennial county superintendent of public education, worked tirelessly to improve the school system. An active county teachers association, organized in 1889 principally by the efforts of Miss Etta Maynor, greatly aided Askew. All, however, had to contend occasionally with irate parents who in 1895 prosecuted Miss Lettie Early, "one of the most active young lady teachers in Bertie," because she switched a tender-fleshed young pupil. A justice of the peace acquitted Miss Early of any violation of the law. Three years later a lengthy paper presented to the teachers association dwelled upon discipline, "the government of the school," which was indispensable for proper classroom instruction.

Before the opening of the fall session of 1900 Superintendent Askew issued a public address to the teachers of the county. He reminded them to maintain law and discipline in the class, to encourage morality and neatness, and to teach thoroughly all subjects required by law. The last included spelling, defining, reading, arithmetic, English grammar and composition, geography, the nature and effect of alcoholic drinks and narcotics, elementary physiology and hygiene, civil government, the history of North Carolina, and the history of the United States. Askew urged teachers to inculcate a "broad sense of patriotism and christian principles" into the minds of the children but strictly avoid "partisan politics and partisan religion. . . ."

By 1905 Bertie schoolchildren faced a four-month term, usually beginning in December when the need for farm labor was minimal. A total of 105 teachers instructed 2,529 pupils in that year. Salaries continued low and discrimination between the races and sexes remained evident. Average monthly salaries were $31.50 and $23.76 for white males and females respectively, and $23.46 and $21.97 for black males and females respectively.

The twentieth century brought rapid improvement to the public school system. In 1916 the county school board decided to employ in the white schools only those teachers who had graduated from high schools "with at least 10 reportable grades" or who offered equivalent credentials. Two years later the board sought money for audiovisual instructional aids. From 1910 to 1920 Bertie reduced the percentage of its illiterate white males from 10.1 to 8.5, ranking in the latter year twenty-second among the state's 100 counties in that regard. Based on five academic and five financial factors, Bertie's white school system ranked thirtieth among the rural white school systems in North Carolina in 1926-1927. In that year the county established a bus transportation network for schoolchildren, and in 1929 the school board declared ineligible to teach any man who gambled, drank, or habitually used profanity and any woman who used profanity, played cards for money, drank, or smoked.

Nonetheless, an assessment of public education in Bertie at the end of the twenties was far from roseate. According to one investigator, "The [white] people of the county as a rule do not favor Negro education in any form" and did nothing to promote such education "except those things demanded by the state." Compulsory school attendance laws proved difficult to enforce for whites and blacks alike. Excessive transportation costs were occasioned by poor roads, a scattered population, and high repair bills for the county vehicles. Teacher turnover was high, estimated at 60 percent annually, as was pupil turnover in an agrarian area characterized by tenant farming. The floating population not only militated against proper instruction but created havoc with school administration. Finally, the low tax base for the county created problems for funding adequately the school system.

Despite racial, demographical, and financial difficulties public education in Bertie made headway. In the third quarter of the twentieth century integration of the schools was accomplished, kindergartens were added, and consolidation of county facilities was realized. From more than 100 schools early in the century, the Bertie system contracted to 56 in 1948 and to 10 by 1976. Encouragingly, an increasing percentage of those graduating from high school seemed intent upon pursuing their education.

Still, there remained much to be accomplished. The county school system ranked next to last in the state in 1976-1977 in the percentage of classroom teachers with graduate certificates and second in the state in the percentage of teachers without prior experience in the classroom. In per pupil expenditures from local funds in 1975-1976 Bertie ranked 138 in a total of 148 educational systems in North Carolina, though with the addition of state and federal funds that ranking improved to 64. Many have utilized private schools or academies for the education of their children, but the vast number of young people remain in the public schools where they must acquire the knowledge and skills that will enable them to make the transition to a modern industrial economy.

For those in the antebellum era who desired to continue their education beyond the classroom, the Bertie Lyceum, organized in 1850, allowed young men in the vicinity of Windsor to enjoy "the benefit to be derived from a free & frequent interchange of opinion on Moral, Scientific & Literary Subjects, and of acquiring an easy mode of expressing ourselves in public without embarrassment. . . ." L. S. Webb chaired the organizational meeting; H. A. Gillam was the first president. During the next two years the lyceum debated such current questions as the propriety of the United States' acquisition of territory from Mexico in 1848 (negative), the wisdom of allowing females to vote equally with males in North Carolina (negative), the necessity of establishing a penitentiary in North Carolina (affirmative), and the desirability of annexing Cuba to the United States (negative).

Although the lyceum faltered within a short time, the Windsor Debating Club emerged to replace it in 1853. After the interruption by the Civil War, the editors of the *Albemarle Times* in 1875 called for a debating society to accompany the drama company, "Phunny Phellows," in Windsor. The editors, who had been active in the creation of the lyceum before the war, contended that a debating club would inspire young men "with confidence," develop their "latent powers," and for those considering a political career promote "that address and elocution which gives a peculiar charm to the consumate orator." The outcome of the editors' proposal is moot, but at the turn of the twentieth century Windsor boasted a Literary and Social Club. However, the coeducational nature of its composition probably furthered more social than literary endeavors.

Those with leisure, ability, and requisite funds indulged their intellectual curiosity by amassing reading libraries. Usually referred to as "parcels" in the early estate records, the size of the holdings amounted to sixty books for Captain Simon Jeffries, who died about 1729, and to over 100 volumes for George Pollock in 1763, the latter described as "the library of a linguist, mus[i]cian, and classical scholar." Before 1783 as many as 60 percent of those for whom inventories or sales of estates exist left books, including Richard Swain, who in 1782 owned among other titles, *Laugh and Be Fat*.

Reading continued to whet and satiate intellectual appetites in the following centuries. Census statistics in 1850 indicate the existence of six law libraries in addition to the various general holdings, and by 1870 the census showed twelve private libraries and three "Sabbath School" libraries that contained 3,600 and 655 volumes respectively. Newspaper advertisements reveal opportunities for Bertie residents to buy the ever popular almanacs, to engage in mail-order, self-improvement study courses, and in 1895 to obtain from the Bee Hive Store in Raleigh ten used books of assorted titles, including classical school readers in French, Latin, Greek, and German, all for one dollar.

In the twentieth century the county library emerged from the efforts of Mrs. L. B. Evans and Mrs. W. T. Tadlock in the 1930s. The Windsor Public Library operated from 1939 to 1942, at which time it became the nucleus of the Bertie County Library. Book stations set up throughout the county were periodically replenished by the county librarian. After almost a quarter century of housing the library in the Windsor Municipal Building, plans were made in 1964 to construct a separate structure for library purposes named the Lawrence Memorial Public Library to honor the W. R. Lawrence family for their contributions to the civic and economic development of Bertie County.

Aiding the diffusion of knowledge in Bertie was the newspaper, the premier means of written public communication. Bertie's earliest paper probably was the Windsor *Journal*, mentioned by the *Raleigh Register* in 1823. Eight years later John Campbell moved from Halifax to Windsor and announced his intention to publish a paper that would support the reelection of Andrew Jackson but would oppose federal encroachment upon state sovereignty. The *Windsor Herald and Bertie County Gazette* appeared in April, 1832, one of twenty-five newspapers published in nineteen towns and cities in North Carolina in that year.

During the last three decades of the nineteenth century several weeklies sprang up in Bertie. The *Albemarle Times* started operations in 1874. Its circulation reached beyond the county to Enfield, Plymouth, Scotland Neck, Hertford, Edenton, Winton, Murfreesboro, Elizabeth City, and Jamestown. The *Times* seemingly discontinued at the end of 1876 when the editors, Patrick H. Winston, Jr., and Moses Gillam, announced their desire to return to their respective professions of law and merchandising. Importantly, delinquent subscribers owed the paper over $1,200, and the editors declared on December 8, 1876, that "Unless the greater part of this money is paid before the two weeks succeeding Christmas have expired, the *Albemarle Times* will expire."

Although the *Times* ceased publication, the following decades witnessed the appearance of other sheets including a Negro paper, the *Home Journal* in 1890-1891, the *Orient*, a mouthpiece of the Democratic party, which thrived for several years after its inception in 1894, and the *Windsor Ledger*. The *Ledger*, starting publication in 1884, was also blatantly Democratic in its political opinion. In 1898 its editor declared, "the rule of the white people is to be the rule of those who glorify the State and give it clean and decent government." Two years later the paper was mailed free to any "white man's club" in the county.

By the beginning of the twentieth century the *Windsor Ledger* had become the county's leading newspaper. However, in 1922 the inauguration of the *Aulander Advance* challenged its supremacy. Four years later the Windsor and Aulander publications merged. The resulting *Ledger-Advance* was published in Aulander and mailed from Windsor. In 1929 Ahoskie publishers J. Roy Parker and J. Mayon Parker bought the paper, renaming it the *Bertie Ledger-Advance*. At about the same time a Windsor-based sheet, the *Bertie News Leader*, briefly appeared, only to be purchased by the Parkers.

In addition to the county newspapers Bertie inhabitants looked to other North Carolina and nearby Virginia publications for information. Edenton papers, beginning with the publication of the *State Gazette of North-Carolina* in 1788, were popular. In addition to taking the *Raleigh Star* in 1842, John B. Williams subscribed to the *American Beacon and Virginia and North Carolina Gazette*, a Norfolk-based paper that cost a rather extravagant $5 per year. In the twentieth century papers from Ahoskie, Williamston, Plymouth, Edenton, Raleigh, and Norfolk supplemented the *Bertie Ledger-Advance*. Other media coverage derived from area radio stations and television reception from Greenville and Washington, North Carolina, and Norfolk, Virginia.

RELIGION

If the early inhabitants of the area that became Bertie embraced any religion, it was probably Quakerism, the only organized religious discipline in North Carolina until 1700. At the beginning of the eighteenth century the provincial government made a determined effort to promote the Church of England or Anglican church, which was the established church of the colony. Legislation in 1701 and 1703 formally implemented that establishment by creating parishes and providing for ministerial support. After 1715 two parishes, St. Paul's and Southwest, served the inhabitants of Chowan Precinct, and from England the Society for the Propagation of the Gospel (SPG) sent missionaries to enlighten benighted Carolinians.

Upon the creation of Bertie in 1722 the assembly designated Southwest Parish to accompany the new precinct but changed its name to Society Parish to honor the SPG. In 1727 the growing population of Bertie caused the legislature to create a second parish for the county, called Northwest Parish, though it was lost to Northampton when that county was formed from Bertie in 1741. In the meantime the SPG encountered difficulty in finding missionaries willing to serve the parishes of North Carolina. Less than fifty Anglican ministers came to the province before the Revolution, primarily because of the low salaries and primitive living conditions, and those who appeared sometimes proved less than worthy characters.

The Reverend John Boyd, who practiced medicine in Virginia before he was ordained in 1732, was the first Anglican missionary to labor in Society Parish. He may have come in response to a plea to the bishop of London in 1726 by Governor Richard Everard. Seeking missionaries for Bertie, Pasquotank, and Bath precincts, the governor wrote, "we are a most heathenish part of America & have no sect amongst us but Quakers who daily increase." Boyd, unfortunately, failed to cope with the stressful conditions that he encountered. Governor Gabriel Johnston referred to him as "one of the Vilest & most Scandalous Persons in the Government," a man found one Sunday at noon "Lying dead Drunk & fast asleep, . . . with his Horse's Bridle tyed to his Leg. . . ." Soon thereafter it was reported that Boyd was dead and that he "died in the same Beastly Manner he lived."

Succeeding Boyd was the Reverend John Holms, whose brief career included a suit against his parishoners in Northwest Parish in 1741 to recover the arrears of his salary. After the departure of Holms ministers from neighboring parishes officiated occasionally in Bertie. The Reverend James Moir from Edgecombe and Northampton counties and the Reverend Daniel Earl from Chowan County visited Bertie in the early 1760s.

William Tryon, called by one Anglican minister "the nursing father of the church," greatly improved the Anglican establishment during his tenure as governor (1765-1771). By 1767 Society Parish again claimed its own minister, the Reverend Thomas Floyd, who was followed in 1770 by the Reverend Francis Johnston. However, the nominal hegemony of the Anglican church in North Carolina ended with the Revolution. Not only was the church discredited by its close association with royal government, but the state constitution of 1776 ended the establishment and provided for religious toleration.

The failure of the Anglican church to achieve the position of supremacy to which it was entitled by law derived in part from the strong dissenting elements in the colony. Among the most prominent dissenters in eastern North Carolina were the Baptists and Methodists. The General Baptists appeared in Bertie perhaps as early as the 1720s and erected the first church built in the county. Originally constructed about 1740, the Sandy Run Church was moved to its present site in Roxobel in 1854. After the mid-eighteenth century the Separate Baptists, originating in New England revivalism and adhering to Calvinistic doctrine, joined the General Baptists. The Separatists took control of the Sandy Run Church, which became one of the original churches of the Kehukee Baptist Association founded in 1769. The Separatists proved superb proselytizers and also founded churches in 1771 at Cashie, about a mile east of Windsor, and in 1789 at Wiccacon Creek under the direction of Jeremiah Dargan and Robert Hendry respectively.

The Methodists in North Carolina made a belated appearance in the colonial era. The Reverend Joseph Pilmore, a Methodist itinerant, first brought John Wesley's message to Carolinians in September, 1772, when he preached at the Currituck County courthouse. Thereafter Methodism made numerous converts in the Albemarle, allowing historian William W. Sweet to call northeastern North Carolina and southeastern Virginia "the cradle of American Methodism." Reinforcing Methodism's prominence in Bertie were the visitations of Francis Asbury, the denomination's premier circuit rider, in the post-Revolutionary days. In late 1783 and in December, 1784, Asbury wrote in his journal that he had preached to considerable congregations in Bertie, Hertford, and Northampton counties.

The Baptists, and to a lesser degree the Methodists, dominated the religious scene in nineteenth-century Bertie, for the Episcopal church never recovered from the effects of the Revolution. It remained dormant

Charles Pettigrew (1744-1807) studied for the ministry and was ordained in London in 1775. He became the rector of St. Paul's Anglican Church in Edenton in 1778. Between 1790 and 1794 he tried to organize the Episcopal Diocese of North Carolina. Though never consecrated, he was elected unofficial bishop of the diocese. His second wife was Mary Lockhart of Scotch Hall, at which they resided from 1794 to 1797.

until 1790 when the Reverend Charles Pettigrew helped to establish the Episcopal Diocese in the state and became its first bishop-elect. Pettigrew was born in Pennsylvania but moved to North Carolina about 1760 and succeeded Daniel Earl as the rector of St. Paul's Parish in Chowan County in 1778. After marrying Mary Lockhart, his second wife, in 1794, Pettigrew lived in her home, Scotch Hall plantation in Bertie County. Upon his death in 1807 the only Episcopal minister in North Carolina was Nathaniel Blount.

Revealing the popularity of the Baptists in Bertie was the fact that the denomination claimed ten of the sixteen churches in the county in 1850. The Methodists followed with four, and the Episcopalians and Free Willers had one each. Boosting the ranks of the Baptists and Methodists was the Second Great Awakening, a national religious revival that began about 1800. Camp meetings, already popular among the Baptists and Methodists, further encouraged religious association and proselytization. William D. Valentine contended that the preaching was "deficient" and the attendance poor at a Methodist gathering (probably) held at Indian Woods in the fall of 1837, but as late as 1858 Frances Gray Pugh wished that her niece could have seen the throng that daily passed Windsor to attend "the protracted meeting over the Bridge at the Cashie [Baptist] Meeting House. . . ."

After the Civil War, in 1870, the Baptists had doubled the number of their churches in the county to twenty and claimed 4,873 communicants. The Methodists still had four churches and the Episcopalians two. The increase in the Baptist churches reflected the rise of Negro congregations after the war. The four churches in Windsor in 1874 included a Baptist congregation over which the Reverend Bryant Lee, also active in politics, presided. Before the Civil War religion appealed to slaves as a means of fraternizing, maintaining their cultural identity, and coping with their bondage. Blacks not only organized their own religious groups but sometimes participated in the meetings of whites, particularly the Baptists. As early as 1773 the black members of the Sandy Run Baptist Church had their own black preachers and were holding their own services. The autonomy of the Baptist congregations, the evangelical spirit of that denomination, and prewar association with the Baptists led to the formation of several Negro Baptist churches in Bertie after 1865.

The dominance of the Baptists remained undisputed in the twentieth century. According to the Census of Religious Bodies in 1936, of the reported 10,326, or 40 percent of Bertie's population, who claimed church membership, 8,742 or 85 percent were affiliated with the Baptist denomination. Methodists constituted 10 percent of the professors of religion, followed distantly by 201 Episcopalians and a scattering of other communicants. Negroes figured prominently in the religious life of the county. Over half the Baptists were blacks; the A.M.E. Zion Church contained 40 percent of the Methodists. A quarter century later the Baptist, Methodist, Episcopal, Pentecostal Holiness, Assembly of God, and Roman Catholic churches held services in the county.

TRANSPORTATION

The topography of Bertie favored the rapid peopling of the county. The many rivers, creeks, and streams allowed easy access to the area as the early settlers plied the waters in craft ranging from canoes and flats to periaugers and small schooners. Residents and travelers, however, often found impediments to navigation, and the county court, acting on authorization granted by the provincial legislature, continuously sought to clear the watercourses of obstructions. Nonetheless, as late as 1874 people interrupted traffic on the Cashie by felling trees into the river, and in 1895 a freshet, representative of those that periodically wreaked havoc in the county, filled the Roanoke River with debris.

Situated on the Albemarle Sound and possessing excellent water arteries to the interior of the county, Bertie was necessarily concerned with shipping facilities. Docks invariably attended private plantations in order that owners might take advantage of waterborne commerce. Ferry sites, too, became locations of landings. In 1782 twenty-five men petitioned the county court that one Thomas Cockran had fenced a road leading to Fry's Ferry, thereby depriving them of their customary privilege of carting goods, particularly fish, to and from the ferry quay.

Public facilities appeared as early as 1739 when the provincial assembly ordered the construction of warehouses to store goods taken in payment of quitrents and taxes and for the inspection of tobacco and other merchantable commodities. Within a decade, however, probably by 1747, the warehouse on the Chowan River had been "burnt down and Destroyed" and the one on the Cashie River had been "lately blown down." After their appearance towns provided public landings. In 1849 the Windsor commissioners let a contract for rebuilding and enlarging the public wharf at the end of King Street. Its cost was unspecified but twelve years later Colerain on the Chowan River rebuilt its wharf for $533.40.

As the early inhabitants of Bertie began to settle away from the water, the need for roads became evident. Charged by law with overseeing the road system, the justices of the county court determined routes and appointed overseers to maintain highways and "bridle paths." Marshlands and low-lying areas rendered maintenance difficult. Consequently, the court received numerous complaints about travel conditions, exemplified by the petition from several persons near Ralph Outlaw's Chapel who claimed that "some Swamp's and Branches in Wett Season's" made the chapel road "unpassable a great part of the year whereby well inclined Christian's are prevented attending the Chappel and Divine Services. . . ." In addition to coping with the foibles of nature, the court in

1735 and 1744 tried to assist those unfamiliar with the surroundings by ordering the marking and posting of roads to and from the courthouse and all public ferries, an action that antedated by twenty years provincial legislation of the same intent.

Like the difficulties of water transport, problems of highway travel continued to beset the county. In 1898 the *Windsor Ledger* declared that "for one-third of the year the roads within five miles of Windsor are impassable for anything but a light buggy and hard even for that." The resulting high transportation costs retarded economic development, particularly that of agriculture, which constituted the foundation of the county's economy. Thus the paper counseled the county commissioners to investigate the matter of improved roads, "which is interesting the entire country outside of Bertie County."

The situation changed little until after the First World War, despite the gubernatorial administration of Locke Craig (1913-1917), a Bertie native living in Buncombe County, who was known as the "Good Roads" governor. According to one report, when Bertie switched from the township system of building and maintaining roads to a county supervisor in 1921, "there was not a creditable road in the county." The change in highway administration plus state financial aid eventually resulted in considerable improvement of the road system in the ensuing years.

Locke Craig (1860-1925), a native of Bertie County, was known as North Carolina's "Good Roads" governor during his administration from 1913 to 1917. In 1915 he established a state highway commission.

41

Where roads intersected watercourses, crossings were effected by fording, bridging, and ferrying. The county court by law directed the placement and construction of bridges. The structures were first built by those men and their slaves who lived close to the bridges, but after legislation in 1756 they could be, and often were, built at county expense by private contractors. According to contracts between the county and those who agreed to build bridges in the eighteenth century, the floor of the average bridge was 5 to 7 feet above the water and the structure had one or two protective rails on each side. If a contractor was dissatisfied with the established fee, he could petition the court "Chearfully and generously to enhance the price for building the bridge," as did Thomas Whitmell in 1771. Whitmell, in erecting a bridge over the Cashie, told the court that he had contracted for such a low price, which was "infinitely short of the intrinsic Value of such a piece of Work," because of his "public Spiritedness." His elegant plea netted him a substantially larger sum of money.

In addition to the usual bridge construction Bertie boasted one of the two drawbridges built in North Carolina before the Revolution. Benjamin Heron's drawbridge over the Northeast Cape Fear north of Wilmington, the first in the colony, has gained more notoriety, but in 1774 the Bertie County court ordered the construction of a drawbridge over the Cashie River at Windsor "in such a manner as not to prevent vessels from going up the head of the Navigation" of the river. Clarification of the construction of the bridge derives from a contract in 1786 by which Thomas Shehon agreed to rebuild the structure. The document specified that the draw of the bridge was to be "26 feet in the Clear" and that "the draws be Hung with 3 Large Iron hinges on each side of the bridge . . . , the draws to be opened with four Iron chains & weights with Iron Sheaves & Rolers. . . . "

Another, and rare, type of bridge construction in colonial North Carolina was the covered bridge, designed primarily to keep the timbers from rotting but also providing shelter and incidentally promoting ghostly and romantic tales. In 1768 the county court decided to contract for the construction of a "hollow bridge" over Wills Quarter Swamp, and Thomas Whitmell completed the task within the year. Covered bridges became increasingly popular in the county and state during the next century, though by 1979 only eighteen such bridges remained standing in North Carolina. Two were in Bertie—one at Rascoe Mill and the other at Hoggard Grist and Saw Mill.

Where waters could not be forded or bridged, ferrying proved necessary to effect a crossing. Ferry authorization also proceeded from the county court, and Bertie waters produced numerous ferry petitions. The liveliest legal dispute concerning ferry keeping in early North Carolina involved Bertie County and a statutory proscription of competiton within ten miles of an established ferry. Henry Baker, awarded a ferry by the Chowan County court before the creation of Bertie in 1722, complained to the General Court of the province in 1724 that Bertie justices permitted William Maule to keep a ferry at approximately the location of Baker's crossing. The General Court remanded the case to the Bertie County court, which found Maule was maintaining the ferry in a "sufficient condition" and upheld Maule's right to continue his operation. The General Court demurred upon receiving Baker's second appeal, and the death of Maule in the meantime concluded the case by 1726.

As in the cases of posting the roads and building the drawbridge, the Bertie justices moved beyond the norms of transportation policy in the area of ferry keeping. Beginning in the 1740s provincial legislation allowed certain counties to permit free ferriage within their bounds during times of public business—elections, musters, court sessions. But in 1771 Bertie justices on their own initiative altered the concept of free ferriage by authorizing Thomas Ballard to buy a flat and ropes at county expense in order to keep a ferry across the Cashie River to Winsdor free at all times as opposed to public times or for "public business." The ferry service continued through 1775, pending the erection of the drawbridge over the river.

The nineteenth century brought spectacular changes in transportation in the United States, particularly by the adaptation of steam power to water and land travel. Steam transportation on North Carolina waters appeared immediately after the end of the War of 1812. The earliest and most successful efforts were made on the Cape Fear River, but in 1818 the Steamboat Company of Edenton contracted for a boat to run between Edenton and Plymouth. By the eve of the Civil War steamers regularly visited Colerain on the Chowan River and doubtlessly navigated the Roanoke and Cashie rivers as well.

After the war steamers were a common sight on Bertie waters. In 1874 the *Bertie* made runs from Windsor to Plymouth three times a week, and by 1888 steamers belonging to the Cashie Navigation Company daily brought passengers and freight to the wharves of Windsor. During the latter year the *Currituck* made two trips weekly from Windsor to Norfolk, a run also made by the *Lucy* in the 1890s, which gave Bertie water access to Richmond, Baltimore, Philadelphia, and New York. Many of the steamers were elegantly fitted for passenger accommodations, serving as excursion vehicles for river cruises or transporting the genteel of the county to Nags Head for summer vacations.

One of the last steamers to serve the county was the *Mayflower*. It was formerly an excursion boat in New Jersey before being purchased by the Branning Manufacturing Company to connect the Wellington & Powellsville Railroad in Windsor with the Norfolk Southern in Plymouth. The *Mayflower* had an ill-starred history, capsizing on its first trip, later sinking at the wharf in Windsor, and finally burning in 1920 at the dock in Plymouth.

By the 1930s regularly scheduled water traffic on the Bertie rivers had ended. The Roanoke, Cashie, and Chowan remained capable of supporting waterborne commerce, but competition from other modes of transportation, principally railroads and trucks, supplanted the slow, sometimes uncertain river trade. After the mid-twentieth century the rivers mostly carried pleasure and fishing craft and occasional pulpwood and oil barges.

The railroad made a somewhat tardy appearance in Bertie, in large measure deterred by the ready availability of water transportation and the difficulty of building over the swamps and pocosins in the county. Although the railroad began to revolutionize transportation in North Carolina from its introduction in the 1830s, Bertie did not reap its benefits until the end of the century. As early as 1874 a proposal was made to extend a line from Petersburg, Virginia, to the Northampton-Bertie area, but the county did not realize rail transportation until 1888, when a logging line was constructed to connect Lewiston and the county farm.

Thereafter interest in railroading increased. In 1892 the county evidenced a desire to attract the proposed Norfolk, Wilmington, and Charleston Railroad to its environs. Voters in Windsor Township cast 511 of 530 ballots in favor of subscribing to stock in the company. Colerain Township was less enthusiastic, though a majority of its voters also supported the proposed railroad. The line did not materialize as many had hoped, but by 1895 the Norfolk and Carolina Railroad cut across the northeastern corner of Bertie, giving service to Aulander.

Subsequently J. W. Branning, president of Branning Manufacturing Company, undertook the construction of the Wellington & Powellsville Railroad, fondly known as the "Walk and Push," in order to promote the lumbering interests of his company in Bertie. In 1898 the firm completed a line from Ahoskie in Hertford County to Windsor. This not only resulted in increased commercial activity for the county seat but by way of connection with the Norfolk and Carolina Railroad made possible a trip from Windsor to Norfolk in four hours.

The Wellington & Powellsville shared Bertie traffic with the Cashie and Chowan Railroad, headquartered in Howard in the county. In 1897 the Cashie and Chowan, a twenty-nine-mile track, carried an assessed value of $40,650, which exceeded that of the Wellington & Powellsville by

$5,500. Thus the railroads greatly expanded the tax base of the county as well as invigorated the economy by means of improved transportation.

Numerous problems attended the appearance of the railroads. Narrow gauge track disrupted traffic with connecting lines. Collisions, such as that on the Cashie and Chowan in January, 1895, between the locomotives "Austin" and "Lewiston," caused considerable damage to track and rolling stock. Windsor citizenry met in 1900 to consider Branning's announcement that the W & P might be discontinued because the competition from river traffic rendered his line unprofitable. And Aulander town ordinances in the early years of the twentieth century forbade trains from interrupting traffic on the streets of the town for more than ten minutes at a time.

The Carolina Southern Railway Company, organized in 1927, absorbed the W & P operation. Serving Windsor, Askewville, and Powellsville, the company laid standard gauge track but terminated passenger service, concentrating instead on a substantial freight traffic that included agricultural produce and timber. Subsequently the Atlantic Coast Line and Seaboard Air Line laid track in the northwest corner of Bertie. Before the merger of the two lines in 1967 the Atlantic Coast Line ran through Aulander and Kelford. The Seaboard Air Line also served Kelford as well as Roxobel, Lewiston, and Woodville.

Supplementing the rail facilities in Bertie in the late twentieth century are a network of roads and proximate air service. Two U.S. highways, 13 and 17, four state highways, and numerous secondary roads support private automobile travel, interstate bus service, and approximately ten trucking companies. Within a seventy-mile radius of Bertie commercial air service is available at Elizabeth City, Rocky Mount, and New Bern. The Tri-County Airport, located in adjoining Northampton County, caters to Bertie, Hertford, and Northampton counties. Clearly Bertie is no longer the "lost province" of the post-World War I era as the county was then characterized by one observer.

TOWNS

Although Bertie is an overwhelmingly rural county, not having any area sufficiently populous to be classified by the federal census as "urban," it contains several communities that vary in size from a few hundred to over two thousand inhabitants. The largest, and oldest, incorporated town is Windsor, the county seat. Other incorporated communities include Aulander, Askewville, Colerain, Kelford, Lewiston, Powellsville, Roxobel, and Woodville. In addition, Merry Hill, Rosemead, and several other unincorporated places enjoy a long and distinctive history. And there have been towns contemplated or begun but lost to antiquity. Wimberly, representing the first attempt to establish a town in Bertie, exemplifies such abortive efforts. Though the assembly in 1752 passed legislation to establish Wimberly, located at Blackman's Landing on Joseph Wimberly's Chowan River plantation, the town failed to survive.

In 1767 the assembly renewed its efforts to erect a town in Bertie by incorporating Windsor at the site of Gray's Landing on the south side of the Cashie River. To secure lots in the town prospective residents were required to construct a house at least 16 feet square within three years of their purchase of land, though by 1774 "Unavoidable Hindrances and disappointments" had prevented so many from completing their buildings that the assembly extended the deadline for another two years. Trustees or directors, designated by law to govern the town, were self-perpetuating, being able to select successors to those of their number who died or retired from office.

Windsor thrived after its inception. By 1773 it contained several "Houses of Entertainment" or taverns, "sundry Stores," and "a good Ferry" to transport persons across the river. These advantages plus its central location in the county prompted the legislature in 1774 to designate Windsor as the county seat, effective in 1775.

In the nineteenth century the commission form of government continued to dominate Windsor life, but the civic process became more democratic. According to a statute in 1817, the town citizenry annually elected three commissioners and a magistrate of the police. The commissioners in turn selected a clerk, treasurer, constable, and overseer of the streets. During the next century and a half the legislature continually expanded the corporate limits of Windsor, which in 1961 permitted the assimilation of the small adjacent community of Bertie, altered the town voting procedures in 1933 to instigate the use of ballots in elections, and changed the form of government to include a mayor.

Though the county seat, Windsor remained a small town, populated in the early 1830s by 160 blacks and 128 whites. Some twenty homes, eight stores, two taverns, two doctors' offices, two lawyers' offices, a printing office, a post office, and several shops constituted the town. Still, Windsor impressed William D. Valentine in 1837 as "the most enlightened spot in Bertie," though he admitted that there were "two or three other flower beds of intelligence," namely Colerain, Woodville, and Britton's Crossroads. Soon, however, Valentine's attitude changed. He recorded in his diary, "Making money, horse racing, common swearing and gambling seem to centre about this village." After a year's residence, Valentine was thoroughly disgusted. He believed that Windsor was "seared in vice and tainted with rude coarse and blackguard sentiments and vulgar manners."

By the turn of the twentieth century Windsor proved a growing, bustling little town. From 427 people in 1870 its population rose to 593 in 1890. During the ensuing decade many brick buildings began to line the streets where few previously stood. A courthouse, "more spacious and magnificent than any in eastern Carolina," appeared "in the stead of the one of our fathers," according to the *Ledger*. Among the brick structures was Leigh's new barber shop, with its new chairs, fine mirror, and marble basis, "as elegantly fitted up as any tonsorial emporium in New York."

The newly emerging brick buildings resulted in part at least from the ravages of fire. Wooden buildings, the accumulation of refuse, and carelessness contributed greatly to devastating conflagrations. In 1888 a blaze caused a property loss of more than $7,000 in Windsor, only one tenth of which was insured. Twelve years later an even more damaging fire, probably caused by a thoughtlessly thrown match, brought together whites and blacks, men and women, townspeople and those from the nearby countryside, in a common effort to save the town.

The town commissioners responded to the second fire by forbidding the construction of wooden buildings in the business district of Windsor. Still the town lacked fire engines, an ample supply of water, and an organized fire-fighting force. The bucket brigade continued to prevail until the early 1920s when the town installed water mains and fire hydrants. By 1939 Windsor had acquired a fire engine and organized a twenty-seven-man volunteer fire department.

Despite the advances made by Windsor at the close of the nineteenth century, the *Ledger* remained dissatisfied with the overwhelming dominance of agriculture in Bertie County. In keeping with the industrialization philosophy of the "New South" advocates, the editor of the paper continually called upon Windsor citizenry to attract industry to the town in order to develop the full economic potential of the area. According to the paper, while Windsor remained contented with its status, prosperous cities in North Carolina had arisen where once there "were unfenced pastures, unmarked save by the beaten paths of swine." Eventually, Windsor realized the hopes of the *Ledger*. In the twentieth century the town became the center of two thirds of the county's manufacturing industry and has been one of the few incorporated areas of Bertie to witness a rising population.

The next most populous town in Bertie County is Aulander. Originally Harmon's Crossroads, the town derived its name from Andrew J. Dunning, a prominent landowner in the area, who wanted to call the town Orlando after the Florida city. Encountering the objections of the postal authorities, Dunning reputedly resorted to an altered spelling that retained the sound of Orlando.

After its incorporation in 1873 Aulander grew rapidly. The town ordinances from 1913 to 1918 reflect the development of a small North Carolina town in the early twentieth century. Facing the need to protect the public health, Aulander commissioners controlled the location of privies and water closets and eventually provided public facilities that were regularly cleaned by town employees. A town ordinance prohibited throwing garbage in the streets or vacant lots because it might attract "country hogs." Periodically the commissioners also met complaints by citizens such as a Mrs. Hollomon who claimed that refuse from a nearby soda fountain ruined her water and produced an offensive odor.

Envisioning traffic problems, the commissioners enacted ordinances forbidding anyone to drive any vehicle or ride any animal faster than ten miles an hour in town. No one was allowed to board trains, moving or stationary, "without business," though "gazing at the passengers to see who is on" was acceptable "business." Subject to fines were persons who obstructed the streets and sidewalks, whether horse traders, vendors, or marble players.

The maintenance of the public peace and the protection of the town inhabitants evoked a number of ordinances. Horses, mules, hogs, and goats were not allowed to run loose. Hogs proved such a nuisance that the commissioners in August, 1913, appointed six men to assist the constable in keeping the animals off the streets and gave them the power to deputize others if they needed assistance. Firearms, fireworks, and other explosives could not be discharged in town except at Christmas when fireworks were permitted only under carefully regulated conditions.

Aulander, like Windsor, feared the ravages of fire. By 1913 the town had a fire company consisting of six men who were instructed "to practice the Fire Engine on Saturday afternoons twice a month from 4 to 5 o'clock" and who were paid 50 cents an hour for their efforts. Ordinances also prohibited the construction of wooden buildings in certain parts of Aulander.

The morals of the community came under the scrutiny of the com-

This street scene is believed to be Aulander near the turn of the twentieth century. It is from a postcard postmarked Aulander, 1907.

missioners. Lewd women plying their trade and men who took advantage of their services were liable to fines. Minors under twenty years of age were forbidden "to play in any game of pool" or to loiter about pool halls. It was unlawful for anyone in town in 1918 to operate a slot machine or other similar gaming device. Also forbidden were Sunday sales of merchandise or drinks except for sickness or burial purposes.

Aulander clearly began to modernize its public facilities in the second decade of the twentieth century. In 1912 the town commissioners moved to secure an artesian well. The following year they tentatively agreed to contract with the Bertie Cotton Oil Company for electric lights but later decided to call a meeting of the town citizenry to discuss the action. Those present at that gathering voted unanimously to adopt the proposition of the commissioners to "install an Electric Lighting System in the Town as soon as practicable." Consequently, Aulander acquired fifty-four lights that illuminated the town each day from sunset to 1:00 A.M. Two years after the installation of the lights the Aulander commissioners also authorized the construction of a sewer system.

After Aulander the size of the incorporated communities drops precipitately, for none contained as many as four hundred residents in 1970. Four of the towns are located in the northwest section of the county in the vicinity of Aulander. Roxobel appeared late in the eighteenth century as Cotten's Cross Roads. Subsequently known as Granbury Cross Roads and Britton's Store, it assumed its current name about 1849, pur-

49

portedly from the suggestion of Frances Norfleet, who had been impressed by her reading of a popular English novel, *Roxobel: A Village Tale*, by Mary Martha Sherwood. Although basically a farming community, Roxobel enoyed a thriving mercantile trade in the nineteenth century. However, in the latter years of the twentieth century the town began to experience a declining population.

About two miles south of Roxobel and three miles northeast of the Roanoke River is Kelford. Originally laid out in 1890 by S. A. Norfleet and named for a fjord in Scotland, Kelford was incorporated in 1893. Almost singularly among Bertie's towns, Kelford evidences a predominantly black population. Like most of the towns in the county, its population has steadily fallen during the middle decades of the twentieth century.

Also in the western part of the county about five miles southeast of Kelford are Lewiston and Woodville. Though separately incorporated in 1881 and 1911 respectively, their boundaries are contiguous, and they are known as the twin towns of Bertie. Woodville derived its name from the home of Whitmell Hill Pugh, which was built in 1801. Lewiston emerged from a post office at Turner's Cross Roads in 1816, and in 1872 took its current name from Watson Lewis, who then served as postmaster. Although Woodville has little industry, Lewiston is a center of manufacturing in Bertie.

In the northeast corner of the county lies Colerain, established by statute in 1794. It was named by its founder, John Campbell, for his home in Coleraine, County Londonderry, Ireland, but in the nineteenth century the post office, established in 1818, dropped the final "e." Located approximately one mile from the Chowan River, Colerain early became a center of fishing, an industry that continues to thrive in its environs. Colerain's population in 1970, 373, represented a 10 percent increase over the previous decade and marked the town as the only one in the county other than Windsor and Askewville that achieved a stable, if not increasing, population growth in the third quarter of the twentieth century.

The remaining incorporated towns, Askewville and Powellsville, are Bertie's smallest. Each registered 247 inhabitants in 1970. But while Powellsville showed a decline in population, Askewville revealed a 26-percent jump over the previous decade. Both towns are named for local families. Powellsville, located in the north central section of the county, was incorporated in 1887. Although settled in the 1890s, Askewville was not incorporated until 1951. Because of its location it has the distinction of being called "the center of the county's tobacco belt."

Beyond Windsor, Aulander, and Lewiston the towns of Bertie may be classified as agricultural residential communities. Heavy industry is rare and most industrial activity is confined to the service trades. The mayor-commission form of government characterizes all the towns. Ofttimes they have few or no full-time public employees and rely upon part-time police and volunteer fire protection. In many cases a disproportionate percentage of the population lies in the forty-five and older age bracket, an indication that the declining population experienced by most of the towns will continue.

THE BERTIE ECONOMY

From the inception of the county the economy of Bertie depended upon its natural resources, of which one of the foremost was fertile land. Hence agriculture dominated the economic development of Bertie. Corn, wheat, and a little tobacco constituted the principal commercial crops of the county in the colonial era, and many raised livestock, particularly hogs, for sale. In addition, farmers planted gardens, perhaps raised a small amount of cotton for home use, and tended ubiquitous orchards from which they derived fruit and drink.

After cotton emerged as the South's premier commercial crop in the nineteenth century, the counties of Bertie, Edgecombe, Martin, Pitt, and Lenoir became a center of cotton cultivation in eastern North Carolina. Although farmers large and small turned to the staple, there were some in Bertie who had reservations about its profitability, chiefly because of the lengthy growing season and the labor-intensive nature of the crop. In the words of one Bertie observer in 1839, "Silk we think is destined to supersede cotton." That was illusory, though in 1860 Bertie produced fifty pounds of silk cocoons or 15 percent of the North Carolina total. On the other hand, in 1860 only Anson, Edgecombe, Halifax, and Pitt counties produced more bales of cotton than Bertie.

CARRYING COTTON TO THE GIN

Bertie was one of the largest cotton-producing counties in North Carolina before the Civil War. This sketch of slaves carrying cotton to the gin appeared in *Harper's New Monthly Magazine* (March, 1854).

Thomas F. Norfleet built Woodbourne in the Roxobel vicinity about 1810. His son Stephen A. Norfleet later received the house and employed progressive farming techniques and slave labor to produce handsome profits for the plantation.

Large plantation interests such as those of Stephen A. Norfleet were responsible for much of the cotton production. Norfleet's accounts books show that he planted 120 acres of cotton in 1856, realizing 88 bales that weighed 37,780 pounds. Encouraged, he sowed 230 acres the following year, only to reap "less than half a crop." However, in 1858 Norfleet's cotton crop yielded 171 bales, weighing 67,500 pounds, "a superior crop" in the words of the planter.

Norfleet's operations also included the production of over 10,000 bushels of corn annually. That product, whose acreage and value always exceeded those of any other crop in the antebellum South, fed animals and people, converted to drink, and sold commercially when necessary. Norfleet also raised wheat and oats. His apple and peach orchards yielded 671 gallons of brandy in 1858. Plums and apricots were less plentiful. The planter annually slaughtered some 300 to 325 hogs, though the animals seldom averaged more than 135 pounds each. On his Woodburne plantation alone in 1858 and 1859 Norfleet netted handsome profits of $10,291 and $9,078 respectively by his calculations, attributable in part to such progressive farming techniques as manuring with guano, composts, and marl and planting red clover and other soil-enriching crops.

53

Comparisons of agricultural statistics in 1860 and 1870 starkly manifest the devastation of the Civil War. The cash value of farms dropped 50 percent during the decade. Before the war Bertie's livestock comprised 1,744 horses, 1,265 mules, 3,558 milk cows, 988 working oxen, 9,705 sheep, and 38,907 hogs. In 1870 those numbers had declined to 1,063, 724, 2,454, 579, 3,453, and 14,100 respectively. Wheat production declined 75 percent, corn and potatoes over 50 percent, wool by 60 percent. Rice slipped from 486 pounds to 60 pounds, though Bertie was one of only thirty-seven counties reporting the crop in 1870.

Worse still was the extensive use of the tenant and sharecrop labor that came to characterize southern farming after the war. An article in the *Albemarle Times* in 1874 lamented the need to use Negro hirelings and tenants who allegedly cultivated crops badly, abused livestock, mistreated implements, and stole without conscience. A correspondent to the *Windsor Ledger* in 1899 called for legal protection to aid farmers against "shiftless tenants" who left without harvesting crops, often in debt to farmers and merchants alike. Since agriculture was the principal industry in eastern North Carolina, "the source of all prosperity" and bearer of the heaviest burden of taxation, it should be protected, according to the writer. Yet, tenants continued to dominate the agricultural scene, managing 46 percent of the Bertie farms in 1910.

The commercial orientation of agriculture began to change in the last years of the nineteenth century. Cotton remained supreme but the ruinous dependence upon one-crop agriculture began to evoke diversification. According to an editorial in 1895 the *Windsor Ledger* "urged the farmers to drop the silly plan of cotton culture years ago. . . . " In the same year a correspondent to the paper from Merry Hill wrote, "Cotton acreage will be curtailed." "Nothing but absolute want," the writer continued, "can teach the Southern farmer, to stop raising such an abundance of cotton to his detriment. Many have nearly arrived at that stage, and are struggling to pull through the mire of their folly. . . . "

In turning from cotton Bertie farmers began to plant peanuts and reconsider tobacco. Already in 1899 farmers harvested 20,822 bushels of peanuts, a harbinger of the dominance of the crop in the twentieth century. Although some tobacco had been raised from the time of the settlement of Bertie, a mere 471 pounds was reported in 1860. However, a half century later Bertie farmers planted 877 acres, and in 1920 the Windsor Redrying Company, which bought, redried, and stored tobacco, was incorporated.

Farmers were so concerned about their future that some supported the Populist reform movement in politics in the 1890s. Others sought improvement by meetings and forums. In 1896 planters from Bertie,

Northampton, and Hertford counties met in Aulander to hold a Farmers Institute during which they discussed such questions as the advisability of growing tobacco in Bertie County, the problems of stock raising, the value of using manure, the possibility of using fertilizer economically, the proper arrangement of farm buildings, and matters of crop rotation. Inventive genius was also at work. In February, 1899, D. A. Askew, a native of Bertie, exhibited his newly patented automatic stock feeder in Windsor.

The twentieth century found agriculture in Bertie undergoing some fundamental changes. Farmers attempted to effect savings by enlarging their holdings. Thus the number of farmers in the county declined from 3,183 in 1910 to 1,477 in 1969. At the same time the size of the average farm rose from 88.7 acres to 131.3 acres.

Mechanized farming, buttressing the trend toward larger but fewer farms, displaced agricultural workers and resulted in a decline in farm employment. In 1962 a total 54.3 percent of the county's work force engaged in some form of agricultural endeavor. During the ensuing ten years Bertie lost 1,630 agricultural jobs, a loss approximating one fourth of the work force.

Mitigating, though not offsetting, the decline in agricultural employment were increased job opportunities in nonagricultural labor. In addition, the number of Bertie inhabitants working beyond the county more than doubled from 1960 to 1970, constituting 21 percent of the county's employed in the latter year. Most worked in neighboring Hertford and Northampton counties, but some commuted as far as Norfolk, Virginia.

Significant change also occurred in Bertie agriculture in the twentieth century when farmers abandoned their dependence upon cotton and diversified their crops. By the 1970s peanuts had not only emerged as the leading money crop in the county but were deemed the "calling card" of the county by the end of the decade. In 1973 the crop accounted for a third of the total value of the leading commercial crops in the county. Tobacco and corn in that order followed closely, however. Soybeans represented the only other significantly remunerative commercial crop, though county farmers also harvested cotton, wheat, oats, potatoes, and hay. In addition livestock, particularly hogs, remained a prominent part of agricultural production and in 1904 accounted for 12 percent of the value of total farm products sold in that year.

Commerce represented another and integral part of the Bertie economy. Merchants early appeared along the watercourses of the county and then in the small communities to cater to the needs of the populace. They often owned and certainly depended upon sloops and schooners engaged in the West Indian and Atlantic coast trade. By 1800 Windsor had become a small but thriving inland shipping center, sometimes referred to as the "Port of Windsor" in public records. Ten ships listed Windsor as home port in the Ship Registry, the largest being a 158-ton schooner equipped for the West Indian trade.

Windsor firms in the antebellum era imported considerable quantities of goods from northern cities. Extant shipping invoices reveal that the schooners *Oregon* and *Cadmus* in 1843 and 1844 respectively left New York bound for Windsor with goods for Biggs and Brother. The schooner *Olivera* departed Norfolk in 1844 for the same destination. Norfolk was also the port of origin for the schooner *John A. Bembry*, bound in 1852 for Windsor with goods for John Freeman & Co. Meanwhile commerce along the Chowan River was not insignificant. The charges assessed by Colerain for the use of its town wharf in 1861 showed that whiskey, nails, coffee, plows, salt, iron, guano, lime, bricks, molasses, bacon, and furniture were prominent imports.

Biggs and Brother regularly stocked the firm's shelves from New York City houses. Purchasing trips in 1843 and 1844 took a representative of the Windsor store to the following among many other New York establishments: Draper & Clark (straw goods and palm leaf hats); Levi Collins, Jr. (looking glasses); Sheldon, Phelps & Co. (hardware, cutlery, and guns); John Savery & Son (hollow ware, stove ware, and ornamental castings); John N. Sayrs (furniture); Gabriel W. Coit (shoes); Collins, Brother, & Co. (books and stationery), Andrew Lester & Co. (dry goods); The Fashionable Umbrella & Parasol Manufactory; George W. Smith (brooms, baskets, woodenware, and mats); Loomis & Lathrop (dry goods); Wood and Sheldon (groceries); R. L. Smith & Henderson (straw goods, English, French, and American bonnets, and French, Italian, and Swiss silk goods); Mrs. G. B. Miller & Co. (tobacco and snuff); Firth & Hall (music and musical merchandise); Wm. H. Cary & Co. (fancy goods and combs); and Holt & Company (flour and meal). Needless to say, the number and assortment of goods available to Bertie County residents from Biggs and Brother seemed boundless.

Among the many merchants who maintained the tradition of Biggs and Brother in Windsor was J. L. Spivey, who at the turn of the twentieth century offered goods ranging from towels "as low as 3¢" and ladies "Mercerized Silk Petticoats worth 75¢ for 49¢" to imitation cut glass and pork meat. Later in the century commercial establishments centered in the towns of Windsor and Aulander and except for those areas tended to be small operations because of the rural nature of the area that they served. Although commercial activity continued to increase, after mid-century a trend toward a smaller number of businesses, both wholesale and retail, with a larger volume of sales became apparent.

Industry in Bertie has always inclined toward the extractive rather than the manufacturing because nature dealt so bountifully with the county. Bertie inhabitants early turned to the water for fish and to the forests for wood and wood products. For two centuries manufacturing barely progressed beyond that of household and the limited operations needed to transform agricultural and extractive products into such finished goods as flour, food, drink, clothing, shingles, and barrel staves. Even in the twentieth century Bertie remained relatively untouched by large-scale manufacturing enterprise, continuing to base its economy principally upon the land and other natural resources.

After utilizing timber for purposes of shelter and warmth, Bertie inhabitants began to consider the possibilities of commercial lumbering and its ancillary manufactured products of barrel staves and shingles. The bountiful supply of oak, gum, cypress, and pine proved amenable. Sawmills abounded early in the county, most likely the pit-saw rig consisting of a pit and platform with a saw projected through a slit in the platform. A log was placed over the pit and a two-man saw team, one in the pit and one straddling the log, would proceed to cut. By the nineteenth century waterwheel mills appeared by which a similar cutting operation was powered by water instead of man.

Also enticing the early Bertie settlers was the naval stores industry. As one traveler said in 1752, one can ride three hours in the county "without seeing anything except Pine Barrens, that is white sand grown up in pine trees, which will hardly produce anything else." Yet, the land was taken and the people made "tar, pitch, and turpentine, wherever they are near enough to a river to load the products on small boats." A petition to the Bertie County court six years later related that "a great Quantity" of tar and pitch annually was carted to Jackson's Landing on the Roanoke River. In 1837 William D. Valentine commented that the means of subsistence for those in the Indian Woods area was tar and turpentine.

Nature also provided Bertie with another of its major industries— fishing. The efforts of John Campbell in the 1740s and his son-in-law Richard Brownrigg, who operated a fishery at Colerain, Campbell's plantation, usually date the origin of the fishing industry in the county. Thereafter notices of fisheries, particularly along the Chowan River, appeared regularly. Elisha Norfleet advertised in the *Edenton Gazette* in 1810 the rental of two fisheries on the Chowan at Point Comfort. Sold at public auction in 1817 was Wood Island, about four acres of land between Cashie and Middle rivers at the head of Albemarle Sound, on which were "Houses and other improvements for two fisheries and sufficient room for two more. . . . "

From as early as the 1740s the fishing industry played an important part in Bertie County's economy. Seen here is a depiction of a night haul on Albemarle Sound from *Harper's Weekly* (September 28, 1861).

Another prominent occupation throughout the years before the Civil War was milling. Gristmills abounded in colonial North Carolina and in Bertie. The county court entertained twenty-eight petitions for such operations between 1758 and 1775. Ofttimes the mills were subjects of controversy. Sixty-four men asked the county court to deny the request of George Ryan for a mill across Herring Run, a branch of Salmon Creek, because it would deprive them of fish usually taken from the stream, and many were poor, "neither able to raise a Sufficiency of meat to support their families, nor able to buy fish for them." In another instance opposition arose to a proposed mill by Whitman Hall on Flag Run, which flowed into the Roanoke River, because the resulting millpond would inundate "rich tendable Land and Low Ground Range."

Thus at mid-nineteenth century major industry in Bertie centered on wood products, fishing, and milling. Of the 54 businesses that annually sold a minimum of $500 worth of goods in 1850, 34 manufactured staves, shingles, or plank, and 6 produced tar and turpentine; of the remaining, 6 were mills and 8 were fisheries. By 1860 at least one coach-making establishment accompanied the fishing, naval stores, and increased milling operations. In addition, seven merchants appeared on the list of manufacturers, probably because they marketed tar, turpentine, and barrel staves that they received from those indebted to them.

After the Civil War large-scale industry inclined slightly more toward the manufacturing. In 1870 a carpenter, wheelwright, two blacksmiths, and two coach makers supplemented the six fisheries, six gristmills, and four sawmills in the county. Also noteworthy was the introduction of steam power (briefly used before the war) in two of the sawmill operations. Still, water power, animal power, and manpower continued to dominate the industrial scene.

Moreover, the extractive industries remained dominant. Fishing thrived during the post-Civil War years. The average catch at Colerain from 1878 to 1883 was 15 million per season, with some individual seine hauls containing as many as a half million herring. The best-known Bertie fishery was Avoca, situated near the mouth of the Chowan River and owned by Dr. W. R. Capehart. In a lengthy article about the fishery in its September 19, 1896, issue, the Windsor newspaper *Orient* drew attention to the 8,000-foot-long, 35-foot-deep seine that was "shot" or set in the water by small steam vessels and retrieved by steam engines on the shore. It was one of the few fisheries at that time operated by steam power.

Seine fishing was hardly confined to Wood Island and Avoca, however. Along the Chowan River were also fisheries at Lazy Hill, Point Comfort, Colerain, Goose Pond, Bull Pond, Mount Gould, Hermitage, Willow Branch, Edenhouse, and Bal Gra. Of course, the Cashie, Roanoke, and smaller streams had fisheries as well. Seine fishing at these places had its

Seine fishing along the Chowan River and Albemarle Sound produced record catches of herring, menhaden, shad, and rock in the nineteenth century. From *Harper's Weekly* (September 28, 1861).

Equipment and patterns of labor at Bertie fisheries changed little over the decades. Compare the landing nets and workers at the Capehart fishery in 1884 on this page with a similar scene from an Albemarle Sound fishery, ca. 1930, on the next page.

drawbacks, among others interfering with transportation. The steamer *Lucy* in 1895 caught its wheel in the net of H. W. Evans, tearing off 200 yards of net and damaging the boat. Moreover, the herring industry began to decline in the late 1890s, causing increased reliance upon shad and rock.

Bertie's commercial fishing industry centered in Colerain in the twentieth century. After its organization in 1927, the Perry-Belch Fish Company (Perry-Wynns Fish Company in 1953) claimed the distinction of being the world's largest freshwater fishery. In addition to producing filleted herring and roe, the company sold fish scraps for fertilizer and animal food and fish oil for paint and soap. Although the luster of its reputation may have diminished slightly, in 1975 the Perry-Wynns Fish Company remained one of Bertie's three largest industrial concerns.

Among others who took advantage of the timber resources of Bertie after the Civil War were J. W. Branning, C. E. Branning, and Horton Corwin, Pennsylvania men who owned Branning Manufacturing Company. Timber from tracts that they purchased in the lower part of the county was taken by rail and barge to mills in Edenton and Columbia. By inaugurating the age of the railroad in Bertie and operating two steamers, *Bertie* and *Mayflower*, Branning Manufacturing provided the rather

isolated county with more extensive contacts with the outside world and
enhanced the market for Bertie agricultural products. At the same time its
extensive operation over a period of a quarter of a century greatly increased employment, enlarged the tax base, and enhanced personal income in the county. Probably no other single business has had such an impact upon Bertie County as Branning Manufacturing.

As the Branning mill began to phase out operations in the first quarter
of the twentieth century, smaller but more permanent and efficient mills
started to appear. In addition to lumbering, forest-oriented industries continued their operations. In 1964 sawmills, veneer and plywood plants, and
cooperage and stave mills added 14.5 percent to the value of total farm
sales. And with 70 percent of the county in a forested state, the wood industry promises to play a major role in the development of the Bertie
economy.

Despite late nineteenth-century editorials in the *Windsor Ledger* extol-
ling the benefits of industry and exhorting the citizenry to join the forces
of the "New South," the only new manufacturing enterprise that appeared in the county seat was B. H. Levi's cigar factory, which opened in
1896. Much lauded by the *Ledger* as a harbinger of the age of industry in
Bertie and portending prosperity for the county, Levi's concern averaged
the production of five hundred cigars a day. In 1897 Levi advertised "The
Bertie Hustler Cigar" and "The Champion of the 19th Century," the latter with a Sumatra wrapper and Havana filler, guaranteed to be the best
5-cent cigar "ever put on the market."

While the nation and state industrialized in the twentieth century, Bertie remained fundamentally agrarian in its economic orientation. In 1927 the county ranked sixty-eighth among the eighty-seven reporting counties in the total value of its industrial output. Its fourteen industrial businesses employed only 394 persons. After mid-century Bertie attempted to attract industry as witnessed by the formation of the Aulander Development Corporation, the Bertie County Development Association, Bertie Industries, Inc., the Colerain Development Corporation, the Lewiston-Woodville Development Corporation, and the Windsor Development Corporation, though such efforts had to overcome the traditional agrarian suspicion that industry would undermine the low-wage scale of agricultural labor.

Attesting to the positive results of the labors of those trying to entice industry to the county was the 46-percent increase in nonagricultural jobs between 1962 and 1972. The traditional leading manufacturing industries in Bertie, food and wood products, declined slightly, while important gains derived mostly from shoes, machinery, and clothes, an indication of the diversification of manufacturing in the county. While most industry (thirteen of the twenty-two major manufacturing firms in the county in 1975) clustered in the vicinity of Windsor, for many years the largest industrial employer was Harrington Manufacturing Company of Lewiston, whose five hundred employees produced farm and industrial machinery. In 1976 Perdue, Inc., a poultry processing plant employing more than a thousand workers, also located at Lewiston.

POLITICS

Within a decade of the appearance of Bertie in 1722 North Carolina ceased to be a proprietary province. In 1729 the crown purchased North and South Carolina, thereby substituting a potentially powerful, energetic imperial government for the relatively weak, inefficient administration of the proprietors. The first royal governor, George Burrington, whose arbitrary and paranoid behavior offended many, proved a favorite among the inhabitants of Bertie. Holding his memory in "Esteem & Veneration," they regretted his departure and replacement by Gabriel Johnston, a young Scotsman seeking to make a fortune in the New World and willing to go to great lengths to realize his ambition.

Land, the most important economic asset of early America, and all that affected its ownership—the land grant process, securing titles, and land taxes called quitrents—provoked many disputes among the naturally litigious population in North Carolina. Soon after his arrival in the colony Governor Johnston demanded that Carolinians pay quitrents punctually and in scarce specie and threatened to dispossess those who were negligent in their payments. Inhabitants of Bertie and neighboring Edgecombe County responded in 1735 with a remonstrance that chastised the governor, saying that they should "not be disquieted in the possession" of their estates, which they "first paid for honestly & afterwards Settled and Improved with much hard Labour from the Barren Woods exposed to the Violent heat of the sun most part of the Year and . . . trusting to what providence would lay in . . . [their] way for food Sometimes a Deer or Bear & sometimes a Racoone & many days nothing. . . ."

Two years later people from the same counties acted upon their previous declaration. They mistakenly assumed that the arrest of a man in Edenton involved the nonpayment of quitrents. An estimated five hundred men, cursing the king and shouting treasonous threats, marched to the town, only to disperse after learning that the case involved another violation of the law and that the prisoner had been liberated. According to Governor Johnston, when writing to the Board of Trade in England, "It is only in these two Precincts that the people have dared to get together in a Body and how to quell them I cannot tell if they should attempt an insurrection against [the] next collection [of quitrents]."

In addition to disputes over land grants and quitrents, the representation controversy from 1746 to 1754 embroiled the county in a provincial dispute. According to custom that derived from proprietary government, the original precincts (later counties) of Albemarle each sent five representatives to the General Assembly. The counties included Perquimans, Pas-

63

quotank, Currituck, and Chowan. Subsequently, by legislative enactment, Bertie and Tyrrell each received five representatives as well, though Bertie relinquished two of them in 1741 upon the creation of Northampton County. Beyond the Albemarle, however, counties were entitled to only two delegates to the assembly.

After Johnston became governor of the province, he attempted to promote the development of the Lower Cape Fear region but faced the opposition of the Albemarle counties with their overweening representation in the legislature. The governor scored a momentary triumph when the Albemarle delegates failed to attend a legislative gathering that Johnston called to meet in Wilmington in November, 1746. At that session the southern assemblymen, orchestrated by Johnston, passed legislation that equalized representation in the assembly at two members per county and located the permanent capital of the colony in New Bern.

Calling the governor's actions a design "to ensnare and entrap" them, the Albemarle counties protested the actions of the assembly as illegal and presented their case to the crown. While the imperial authorities considered the matter in their usual dilatory manner, the Albemarle counties refused to send delegates to subsequent sessions of the legislature or to obey laws passed by the assembly. The result was civil conflict that bordered on anarchy, at least according to Moravian Bishop August Spangenberg in 1752. Only after Johnston's death and the appointment of a new governor, Arthur Dobbs, did the crown resolve the disagreement. Following the advice of his attorney and solicitor general, who declared that the representation act of 1746 appeared to have been passed "by management precipitation & surprise," the king instructed Dobbs to void the objectionable laws of the 1746 assembly and restore the system of representation that originally had existed.

From the inception of the county in 1722 to the dissolution of the last royal assembly in 1775, Bertie sent thirty-nine representatives to the legislature. Only eight served more than one term. Isaac Hill, Arthur Williams, and John Campbell were elected on three occasions. No one represented the county for more than three terms, a remarkable statistic in an era of deferential politics but one that probably reflected lengthy assembly sessions, a mobile population, and Bertie's loss of land so as to form Tyrrell, Edgecombe, Northampton, and Hertford counties. Moreover, some of the representatives, for example, Dr. Robert Lenox and Moses Houston, had multiple county residences and by law could serve any county in which they owned property. And, of course, families, if not individuals, dominated the political scene. Isaac, Benjamin, and John Hill, Lillington and James Lockhart, George, John, and Benjamin Wynns, and four members of the famed Pollock family composed almost a third of the representatives from Bertie, and they account only for like family surnames and not others who were related by marriage.

In the colonial era the most active and prominent Bertie politician was John Campbell. Probably a native of the town of Coleraine in northern Ireland, Campbell had purchased land in Bertie in 1737 and established a mercantile business in Edenton by 1743. Although he represented Chowan County in the assembly in 1744, he moved to Lazy Hill plantation on the Chowan River in Bertie and continued his political career in that county. Bertie sent Campbell to the assembly in 1754, at which time he served as speaker of that body for two successive years. Ill health and the need to care for his manifold private interests interrupted his political career for a decade, but he returned to the assembly in 1767 and again in 1773. An appointment as commissioner for the port of Roanoke in 1752, as an assistant judge in 1756, and as mail contractor in 1757 revealed the political influence and prestige of Campbell, who closed his public career with extensive service in North Carolina's provincial congresses.

Assemblymen like Campbell ofttimes represented the influence of the "courthouse ring" in the counties, a group of officials who dominated politics from the county court through the highest echelons of the provincial government. Overseeing county government were the justices of the peace. Appointed by the governor, these magistrates ranged in number from thirteen to eighteen in Bertie before the Revolution. Their duties were manifold, running the gamut from settling neighborly altercations to taking lists of taxable persons, but their principal power derived from constituting the court that decided lawsuits, created roads and ferries, licensed taverns, appointed minor county officials, and generally transacted the affairs of local government.

The justices invariably represented the eminent of the county. For example, in the 1760s the county commissions included John Campbell, John Dawson, Cullen Pollock, Edward Rasor, Lillington Lockhart, Humphry Nichols, David Standley, and William Gray, men of wealth and family. Occasionally, however, the magistrates exceeded the bounds of propriety. The assembly in 1733 complained of "Oppressive Magistrates in Bertie and Beaufort, divers whereof are persons of very ill Fame and Character . . . ." And ten years later the provincial council recommended that Peter West, a Bertie justice, be struck from the county commission for tendering "an oath to several persons in very obscene terms" and "in a very irregular extra judicial manner. . . ."

On the local scene one of the issues that sometimes divided sentiment and the "courthouse ring" was the location of the county courthouse. The courthouses, with their accompanying structures, the jails and stocks, were central to county politics, and the location of the buildings was a prime concern of the populace. Preferably, the courthouse should be situated in the center of the county with suitable access by land and water if possible. However, the constant division of the counties and the machinations of local land speculators resulted in heated controversy over courthouse locations in the eighteenth century.

After the creation of Bertie in 1722, the courthouse, prison, and stocks were built at what is now Saint Johns in Hertford County. Upon the establishment of Northampton County in 1741, the site necessarily changed. Acrimonious debate surrounded the selection of a new location for the county buildings. Compounding the problem was the ongoing construction of a new courthouse by Noah Pridham at the old location. Thus the county court had to recompense Pridham for the work already completed as well as find a new site. A new contract was issued for constructing the courthouse on the south side of Stony Creek at Joseph Barradial's plantation, but a succeeding court in 1742 changed the site to Red Bud Branch. The issue went to the General Court of the province, but that body dismissed the case. In 1743 the General Assembly intervened by legislation that directed that the courthouse be located between Cashie Bridge and Wills Quarter Bridge. The court finally settled upon a site on James Castellaw's plantation near his mill and the county warehouse on the Cashie River. To conclude the matter the contractor for the Stony Creek site was paid for his work and the courthouse on Castellaw's land was completed and occupied by November, 1744.

Thirty years later the General Assembly chose to relocate the seat of government in Windsor, the newly created town at Gray's Landing on the Cashie River. According to a petition by numerous inhabitants of the county to the legislature in 1773, not only was Windsor "very conveniently situated and nearly in the center of the County," but the location of the current courthouse lacked "Houses of Entertainment" for those who attended court, and the courthouse was "so rotten & decayed by age" that it was beyond repair. The advantages of Windsor were undeniable. Legislation in 1774 designated it the seat of government, and the town remained the county seat thereafter.

Diverting attention from local politics were the differences in the 1760s between Great Britain and the American colonies that mounted to crisis proportions in the next decade. After the passage of the Tea Act by Parliament in 1773, the Boston Tea Party later in the year, and the parliamentary response in the form of the Intolerable Acts in 1774, Americans convened in a Continental Congress in Philadelphia to protest the arbitrary British measures. In order to select delegates to the Continental Congress North Carolina held the first of five provincial congresses in August, 1774. At that time the provincial congress also suggested the organization of safety committees in the towns and counties of the colony. As the rift between colonies and mother country widened and the Revolutionary War approached, the succeeding provincial congresses prepared for the conflict. In 1776 the fourth congress adopted a resolution to declare independence from Britain; later in the year the fifth drafted a constitution for the state of North Carolina that inaugurated a formal, independent government in 1777.

Fittingly representing Bertie in the First Provincial Congress was John Campbell, who returned to the three succeeding congresses. At the second congress David Standley, a justice of the peace and sheriff of Bertie, and John Johnston joined Campbell. Destined for a career in state politics, Johnston, like Campbell, also served in four congresses. Other notables from Bertie who were elected to more than one congress were Charles Jacocks and Zedikiah Stone, father of future state governor David Stone and a noteworthy politician in his own right.

After the confrontation between British soldiers and minutemen at Lexington and Concord in Massachusetts in April, 1775, war seemed a distinct possibility. The Third Provincial Congress prepared to raise minutemen in North Carolina, requiring two companies from Bertie that would be commanded by Colonel Thomas Whitmell and Lieutenant Colonel Thomas Pugh. And while Bertie contributed to the successful patriot cause, evidence suggests that many in the county were reluctant to break with England. The county did not seem to be a vigorous participant in the early proceedings that led to revolution, and after the start of the war Bertie was a center of an extensive loyalist plot called the Llewelyn conspiracy. Heading the affair was John Llewelyn, prominent Martin County planter, but the cabal had deep roots in Bertie and other counties in the northeast area of the state. The conspiracy, representing a mixture of devotion to the Anglican church, personal animosities, and loyalty to the crown, posed a serious threat to the new state government before it was discovered and thwarted in 1777.

One of the leaders in the Llewelyn conspiracy and heading the loyalist effort in Bertie was William Brimage. Owning thirty slaves and 10,000 acres of land in North Carolina and holding appointments as a provincial vice-admiralty judge and crown prosecuting attorney for Bertie County, Brimage was offered an active role in the patriot cause by his election to the Third Provincial Congress. He evidenced his political sympathies at that time by his failure to attend the congress. Upon the revelation of the Llewelyn plot Brimage tried to leave the province but was captured and imprisoned in Edenton where he "was chained down to the Floor" of the jail. Governor Richard Caswell refused his bail, believing Brimage was "one of the powers of [the] diabolical plan" of the tories. Acquitted of charges of treason, Brimage fled to New York, went to South Carolina upon Cornwallis's invasion of that state, and left for England in 1782 at the evacuation of Charleston. There he remained as one of the many unhappy American exiles while his wife and family continued to live on their plantation in Bertie County.

During the latter days of the Revolutionary struggle the thirteen states united under a government created by a constitution called the Articles of Confederation. While the majority of North Carolinians, jealous of the prerogatives of the states, appreciated the weak central government established by the Articles, so-called "Federalists" in the state and throughout the country believed that the national government was inadequate to cope with the demands of foreign and domestic policy. A successful effort to replace the Articles began with the drafting of the federal Constitution in 1787 and culminated with its implementation in 1789. In the Hillsborough Constitutional Convention of 1788 North Carolina at first refused to ratify the federal Constitution, but the successful start of the new United States, the election of George Washington as president, and the realization of the economic burdens of remaining outside the Union among other considerations convinced a second convention meeting in Fayetteville in 1789 to overturn the earlier decision and vote to join the United States.

From the outset Bertie supported the federal Constitution. Its mercantile and commercial farming interests that derived from the county's proximity to water and worldly trade prompted Bertie delegates at both state conventions to vote to ratify the Constitution. The county elected five delegates to each meeting, but only William J. Dawson, John Johnston, Andrew Oliver, and David Turner appeared in Hillsborough and Francis Pugh and David Stone in Fayetteville the following year. All were men of property and prominent social standing. Some, Oliver and Turner, for example, had extensive experience in state politics as members of the legislature; others, Dawson and particularly Stone, were launching their political careers.

From the advent of the new nation to the Civil War Bertie usually boasted a voice in state political affairs. David Stone, of course, was Bertie's most successful politician, holding numerous state offices, including the governorship, and representing North Carolina in both houses of the national Congress. Other Bertie natives who went to the House of Representatives were George Outlaw, who also served as speaker of the state Senate from 1812 to 1814, Joseph H. Bryan, Kenneth Rayner, and David Outlaw. Eight Bertie residents—Jonathan Jacocks, Stark Armistead, Whitmell H. Pugh, Robert C. Watson, Richard O. Britton, Lewis Bond, William A. Ferguson, and Patrick H. Winston, Jr.—sat on the

Patrick H. Winston, Jr. (1820-1886), was patriarch of one of Bertie County's most distinguished families. A Windsor lawyer, he was father of George T. Winston, president of both the University of North Carolina, 1891-1896, and the Agricultural and Mechanical College (North Carolina State University) at Raleigh, 1899-1908, and of Francis D. Winston, lieutenant governor, 1905-1909. Two other sons were also noted jurists. From Robert W. Winston, *It's a Far Cry* (New York: Henry Holt and Co., 1937), opposite p. 54.

Council of State, the seven-man advisory board for the governor that the legislature elected annually, and William H. Mhoon was state treasurer from 1831 to 1835.

As the new nation emerged in the early 1790s, two political parties arose that commanded the attention and eventually the allegiance of adherents throughout the country. The Federalist party, which identified with the Washington administration, signified wealth, centralized government, and Anglophilism. North Carolina, however, gravitated to the opposite party, the Jeffersonian Republicans, whose association with the South, agrarianism, suspicion of centralized government and high finance, and Francophilism endeared it to the majority in the state. The Franco-American War of 1798 and the determined efforts of Federalist William R. Davie temporarily revived the Federalists in North Carolina, but the Jeffersonians regrouped, secured the state for Jefferson in the presidential election of 1800, and dominated state politics for the next decade. Some dissatisfaction with President James Madison's conduct of the War of 1812 brought a brief resurgence in the Federalists' ranks, though after the war the party collapsed as a national organization.

Bertie politics early showed the influence of David Stone and the Edenton Federalists, a clique led by Samuel Johnston and James Iredell. When Stone, after election to the House of Commons from 1790 to 1795 and three years service as judge of the Superior Court of Law and Equity, sought election from the Edenton District to the House of Representatives in Washington, he tendered his thanks to Iredell for that jurist's assistance in his campaign. Doubtless Stone's political inclinations had earlier been colored by his association with Davie, the epitome of Federalism in North Carolina. Stone won the election by unseating incumbent Demsey Burgess of Camden County and triumphed again in 1800.

The Bertie congressman disappointed his Federalist supporters with a pro-Republican voting record in Washington that placed him among the

Hope Plantation, which has recently been restored, was the home of Governor David Stone (1770-1818). Stone began his career as a staunch supporter of the federal Constitution and the Federalist party, but by the early 1800s he had become a Jeffersonian Republican.

contenders for a United States Senate seat in 1800. Although Stone reportedly did not seek the post, he won election on the first ballot cast by the state legislature, defeating his former mentor Davie by a 94 to 72 margin. Before resigning his seat in the House of Representatives, however, Stone participated in the controversial presidential election of 1800 in which the house was required to select a victor. While the Federalists usually supported Aaron Burr, the Republicans championed Jefferson. On each of the thirty-six ballots necessary to determine the winner, Stone voted for Jefferson, who emerged as the third president of the United States.

After serving one term in the Senate, Stone, a confirmed Republican, returned to North Carolina and assumed a judiciary post to which he was elected by the Republican-dominated state legislature. Two years later, in 1808, he resigned to accept the governorship of the state that had been conferred upon him by the legislature. Reelected for another term the following year, Stone became the only native and resident of Bertie County during the nineteenth and twentieth centuries to serve as governor of the state.

Stone unhesitatingly supported the Republican presidential nominee, James Madison, who succeeded Jefferson in 1809. As governor, Stone relayed a congratulatory message from the General Assembly to the president, saying that "there was not found in the Legislature of this State a single individual disposed to withhold a declaration of increasing confidence in our Chief Magistrate . . . . " He added, "it affords me most sincere gratification to be the instrument for conveying to you the undivided approbation of so respectable a portion of your fellow-citizens."

After serving two terms as governor, Stone moved again to the state legislature where he became embroiled in the controversy involving the selection of presidential electors from North Carolina. The federal census of 1810 showed an increase in the state's population that would allow it an additional electoral vote in the election of 1812. Since Congress had failed to determine the reapportionment of congressional representation, and hence electoral votes, among the states by the time that the North Carolina legislature convened in 1811, that body decided to repeal the law that divided the state into electoral districts and vest the choice of presidential electors in the assembly. Since the Republicans controlled the legislature, that meant a solid bloc of Republican electoral votes would be cast for the party's candidate, James Madison, in 1812.

Federalists looked upon the law as a blatant political measure designed to deprive them of possible electoral votes that would have resulted from district balloting. Stone replied to their criticism in three articles printed in the Raleigh *Star*, under the name "North Caroliniana," saying that the election law gave North Carolina its "due and Constitutional weight," which had been wanting while the "federal minority . . . divide[d] the electoral vote in 1796, 1800, 1804, and 1808." Although the Federalists charged in response that the law was "tyrannical," "unrepublican," and a cheap "electioneering trick" to prop up the declining fortunes of President Madison, the Republicans prevailed for the moment. Taking cognizance of the criticism, the Republicans, despite efforts to the contrary by Stone, eventually relented by repealing the law and instituting the popular presidential vote after denying a Federalist attempt to restore the district electoral system.

Though mildly chastened, the Republicans remained in control of the legislature in 1812. They elected Stone to succeed Jesse Franklin in the United States Senate, determined the speaker of the House of Commons, and chose George Outlaw of Bertie to preside over the state Senate. Outlaw, somewhat in the shadow of Stone, was born near Windsor and educated in Bertie; he engaged in farming and mercantile endeavors. He embarked on his career in state politics by serving in the House of Commons in 1796-1797, after which he moved to the state Senate where he represented Bertie for several terms beginning in 1802. Outlaw continued as speaker of that body in 1813 and 1814, and a decade later he briefly sat

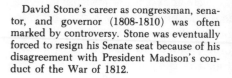
David Stone's career as congressman, senator, and governor (1808-1810) was often marked by controversy. Stone was eventually forced to resign his Senate seat because of his disagreement with President Madison's conduct of the War of 1812.

in the United States Congress to fill the unexpired term of Hutchins G. Burton.

In the meantime the War of 1812 superseded all political questions. After two decades of British depredations to American shipping and slights visited upon the honor of the country, Madison and the Congress opted for war to redress the nation's grievances. Bertie Republicans supported the American position. In November, 1811, a meeting of prominent members of the party at the courthouse in Windsor noted the "awful crisis which overclouds our political horizon." Though they deplored "the anticipated evils of war," they preferred war "with all its horrors, to submission without a struggle" and pledged "their lives, their fortunes and sacred honor to support the government" in whatever course it chose to secure the nation from transgressions by the British.

After the declaration of war in June, 1812, North Carolina and Bertie supported the conflict by sending troops. The effectiveness of Bertie's troops was suspect, for the county's militia in 1810 was characterized as "without discipline" and "inferior in order and appearance" to that of Chowan. But that did not dampen enthusiasm for the war in Bertie. At the Fourth of July celebration in 1812, among the twenty toasts offered at the festivities were those to the war, the president, the memory of George Washington, the army, the navy, North Carolina militia and volunteers, and "The genius of American Independence."

In turn for the state's support of the war the national government did little to help North Carolina. The seacoast remained unprotected in spite of pleas for assistance. When a British fleet appeared at Ocracoke in July, 1813, and landed men in the area, the coastal districts panicked. Although the British departed with little incident in less than a week, the incursion and lack of federal commitment to North Carolina's troops and defense elicited considerable criticism of "Mr. Madison's War."

Exemplifying the discontent within the state was David Stone, whose conduct made him a controversial figure soon after the war began. The senator voted against several measures passed by Congress to prosecute the war. By August, 1813, "Republican meetings" in Bertie and proximate counties expressed "public indignation" at this "apostacy from the Republican principles upon which he had been elected." A gathering in Windsor on August 12 resolved to view Stone's conduct with "indignant disapprobation" for his "opposition to the dearest interest of our Country" and concluded that his votes were so inconsistent with the sentiment he professed before his election as senator that they could only be construed as "emanations of a sacrifice on the altar of Ambition or Corruption." The state legislature evidenced its displeasure with Stone in December, 1813, when both chambers passed resolutions of censure against the senator.

When Stone later visited Raleigh, he intended to resign his office. However, he found partisan politics and war excitement so feverish that he was reluctant to place in the hands of the legislature "so important a trust as the appointing [of] a Senator." Probably, too, he waited for a change in political opinion in the legislature that never materialized. Thus, the following year Stone relinquished his post, citing the "strange . . . war measures" of the administration that threatened to divide, bankrupt, and ruin the country as his reasons for opposing Madison and the Congress. The senator admitted, "I am conscious I possess a very fallible judgment, but which, such as it is, must be my guide in the performance of public duty, entirely independent and uncontrolled by party." As the *National Intelligencer* opined, no one could impugn the character and integrity of Stone.

Although Stone departed political life, Bertie retained its influence in state political circles. In the congressional elections of 1815 Joseph H. Bryan of Bertie polled 55 percent of the votes in the second district to defeat former congressman Demsey Burgess. Bryan won on the strength of his home county, carrying Bertie by 881 to 21, while losing each of the other three counties in the district. Born in Windsor, he served several terms in the House of Commons, later became an active and able trustee of the University of North Carolina, and won reelection to Congress without opposition in 1817 only to retire from politics after his second term in office.

By 1820 the Republicans dominated the national scene as the Federalists, embarrassed by their opposition to the War of 1812 and their overwhelming electoral loss in 1816, disbanded as a national organization. Unopposed in 1820, Monroe won reelection in a lackadaisical campaign that saw only 148 Bertie residents go to the polls. Four years later, however, a spirited, partisan political atmosphere more than quadrupled that number of voters.

In 1824 the Republican party splintered in attempting to find a successor to Monroe. Four candidates, John Q. Adams, Henry Clay, William Crawford, and Andrew Jackson, offered themselves for the presidency. In North Carolina the contest was limited to Crawford of Georgia and Jackson of Tennessee, the latter running on the People's Ticket with John C. Calhoun of South Carolina as his vice-presidential choice. Crawford outpolled Jackson in Bertie by 353 to 269, but the People's Ticket carried the state by almost 5,000 votes. Throughout the nation, the vote was so divided that no candidate received a majority of the electoral ballots and the House of Representatives was forced to decide the outcome between Jackson, Adams, and Crawford.

A few days after the election of 1824 the North Carolina legislature convened. Although the People's Ticket had prevailed in the presidential contest, Jacksonians in state politics fared poorly. Editors of the *Raleigh Register*, a leading Crawford paper, won reelection as state printers, Nathaniel Macon returned to the United States Senate, and Congressman Hutchins G. Burton, who had voted for Crawford in the congressional caucus in Washington, was the legislative favorite in the contest for governor.

Because Burton resigned to accept the governorship of the state, the second district held a special election to fill his vacancy. George Outlaw of Bertie and Willis Alston, the longtime representative from Halifax, campaigned for the seat. A major issue was the selection of the president since the House of Representatives had yet to fulfill its constitutional obligation to elect the president. Outlaw promised to support Crawford; Alston agreed to vote for Jackson. The result was a victory for Outlaw by a vote of 633 to 450.

Adams, the New Englander, subsequently proved the congressional choice for the presidency, and North Carolina politics underwent realignment. Crawford's popularity diminished noticeably. Jackson's supporters, counting on the general's strong showing in 1824, Calhoun's support, and apathy toward Adams, the northerner, organized effectively and campaigned strenuously. Touting Jackson as Jefferson's successor, the old Republicans, or Democrats as they were eventually called, and Old Hickory swept to victory in the state and nation in 1828.

Opposition to Jackson's high-handed conduct as president quickly arose in the state and throughout the country and culminated in the emergence of the Whig party by the early 1830s. The Whigs traditionally have been described as an anti-Jackson party. The president's attempt to destroy the national bank by removing governmental deposits particularly angered North Carolinians and became a focal point of opposition to Jackson. Also consequential were Jackson's ostensible support for the protective tariff and his alienation of John Branch of Halifax, North Carolina, the secretary of the navy whom Jackson had forced to resign in the aftermath of the Peggy Eaton affair. In turn the Branch faction in North Carolina was greatly influenced by John C. Calhoun and his adherents in the state who had reasons of their own, arising especially from the elevation of Martin Van Buren in Jackson's administration, to oppose Old Hickory. Indeed, it appeared that the rise of the Whigs in the South resulted more from anti-Van Buren sentiment than antagonism toward Jackson, as the populace for the most part retained a genuine appreciation for Jackson while he was president but deserted the Democrats in 1836 when Van Buren sought to succeed the Tennessean.

In any event an amalgam of political opinion in North Carolina, ofttimes encompassing both sides of major political issues of the day, coalesced into a new political party called the Whigs, which advocated a strong state government that would actively promote education and internal improvements. As early as August, 1831, Bertie evidenced its political proclivities when a "committee appointed by respectable citizens" in the county invited John Branch to a dinner in his honor in Windsor. In the election of the following year many who opposed the nomination of Martin Van Buren as the vice-presidential candidate of the Democratic party became leaders of the Whig party. By 1835, when North Carolina held a constitutional convention, the Whigs had organized sufficiently to challenge Democratic hegemony throughout the state.

Coincidental with nascent Whiggism was the controversy in North Carolina over a proposed convention to alter the constitution of 1776. Although the original document was brief, inflexible, and undemocratic in light of subsequent developments, Bertie and the eastern counties generally opposed any changes. Westerners, seeking more influence in state politics, just as ardently championed a convention. While Bertie's vote of 315 to 96 against the convention in the 1835 referendum fairly accurately reflected sentiment in the East, a similar majority on the other side of the question from the more populous West carried the day for the proponents of the convention.

Denoting the changing political sentiment in the county were the representatives to the Constitutional Convention of 1835. David Outlaw was a Whig; Joseph B. G. Roulhac an independent. The labors of the convention, despite several democratic reform proposals, apparently confirmed the fears of Bertie and the eastern counties, for they voiced overwhelming opposition to the proposed amendments to the constitution. Nevertheless, the West, again with a decisive majority, approved the amendments and the constitution was altered accordingly.

Once the controversy over the state constitution had been settled, the Democrats and Whigs earnestly began to vie for control of state politics. The Whigs not only provided an alternative to the Democrats in North Carolina, but they organized throughout the United States, thereby allowing local adherents to identify with the national party. For the first time since the days of the Federalists and Jeffersonian Republicans a viable two-party political system existed in the country. The political developments greatly affected the Bertie scene. One observer in Windsor remarked in 1838, "Every fellow who can read a newspaper is a politician. Much sharp political discussion heats feeling into hostility and personal bickering. Party spirit carries away the [rational] man." Political differences frequently resulted in fights or duels.

Although the Democrats won the elections of 1836 in Bertie, by 1838 the Whigs had checked the Jacksonians in the county. William W. Cherry, the Whig candidate for the state Senate, led the party ticket to a resounding victory. By his exertions more than any other according to one Windsor resident, the Whigs succeeded in revolutionizing the county. Cherry was a "great stump orator, a most bitterly formidable antagonist, and the best common-sense talker in all this part of the country." Marring the Whig triumph, however, was a man "shot horribly bad to pieces" when loading a cannon to celebrate the victory.

The election returns in the gubernatorial contests also revealed the shift to Whiggism in Bertie. In 1838 Edward Dudley led a subsequent parade of Whig victories that did not end until 1856, though the state returned to the Democratic fold at mid-century. After a brief interval Bertie again cast its vote for a Whig, John Pool, in 1860, but by that time the Democrats had a firm grasp on the gubernatorial office and John W. Ellis won the election.

Bertie Whigs were also prominent in the contests in the county's congressional electoral district. After illness had prevented George Outlaw from running for reelection in 1824, a succession of Democrats from Halifax—Willis Alston, John Branch, and Jesse A. Bynum—controlled the district's congressional seat. By 1838 the district, like Bertie County, embraced the Whigs and sent Kenneth Rayner to Congress. Born in Bertie in 1808, Rayner studied law, joined the bar, and moved to Hertford County. He served in Congress for three terms, from 1839 to 1845, at the end of which time he declined renomination. Still, he remained active in local politics, and after the Civil War, as a Republican, served as a court commissioner of the *Alabama* claims and as solicitor of the United States Treasury from 1877 until he died in 1884.

Kenneth Rayner (1808-1884), a native of Bertie, served three terms in Congress as a Whig before the Civil War. When the Whig party disintegrated in the 1850s, Rayner briefly joined the Know-Nothing party. After the war he became a Republican.

The Whigs briefly relinquished the district in the election of 1844 but returned to power two years later on the strength of the candidacy of David Outlaw, resident of Bertie. A cousin of former congressman George Outlaw, David Outlaw was born in 1806, attended schools and academies in Bertie, was graduated from the University of North Carolina, and commenced a law practice in Windsor in 1825. The county elected him to the state assembly from 1831 to 1834 and as one of its delegates to the Constitutional Convention in 1835, after which he became solicitor of the First Judicial District from 1836 to 1844. He was a delegate to the Whig national convention in Baltimore in 1844.

Like many who undertook public service far from home, Outlaw evidenced homesickness. "A seat in Congress," he wrote his wife, "may be pleasant to some men, but I assure you it has but little attraction for me, and I feel more like I was going to a funeral, than to enjoy a political triumph." Later Outlaw instructed his wife to tell their children that he missed them, "though they did sometimes annoy me when I was in a bad humour, with their noise." Still, Outlaw adjusted well to his new life, leading his wife to write during his third term, "Well, I see no chance for us ever to live together again but I shall never ask you again not to be a candidate & I will pray for resignation to my lot in life."

Not surprisingly, the congressman was also quickly disillusioned about the nature of national politics. He observed in December, 1847, "The virtue which distinguishes our revolutionary ancestors is gone. Congress is

77

filled not with patriots but mere politicians eager in the race of power and popularity." Subsequently, Outlaw declared that the conduct of Congress "is disgraceful" and that he would not be surprised to see a military government ensue. Indeed, his choice and that of the Whig party for the presidency in 1848 was General Zachary Taylor, who had compiled a distinguished record in the Mexican-American War. But Outlaw in principle feared the military man in civil office. Said he, "The example is a dangerous one, it has proved injurious in other governments, and must have a similar effect here." Still, it was "astonishing what a rage there is for military men in the country. Courage is looked upon as the highest virtue." It seemed to the congressman that the eagerness with which the populace sought courage would lead to the conclusion that the United States was a nation of cowards.

Outlaw remained in Congress to witness the election of Taylor, the death of the president and the succession of Millard Fillmore in 1850, and the crisis over slavery at mid-century generated by the admission of California as a free state. Although the Compromise of 1850 temporarily healed the breach, the "slavery agitation" greatly distressed the Bertie congressman who felt that it was "the only rock upon which we are likely to split." If the nation divided over that issue, he foresaw "a scene of misery, woe, and desolation of which the annals of the world can scarcely furnish any parallel." The agitators who "pushed things to extremes" mistakenly thought that they could control events. Instead, those who tried "to make the people of the South hate those of the North" as enemies or traitors to their country jeopardized "the cause of human freedom, for if our experiment of a republican form of government fails, it is idle to expect it to succeed any where."

The Bertie congressman lived to endure the tragedy of the civil conflict that he had sadly predicted. Like Winfield Scott, the Whig nominee for the presidency in 1852 whom he reluctantly supported in the face of mounting southern opposition, Outlaw was defeated in the election of 1852. Even so, he returned to Bertie to achieve a distinguished record of public service. After representing the county in the lower house of the state legislature from 1854 to 1859, he moved to the state Senate in 1860 where he also served during the war years of 1862 to 1864 and the Reconstruction years of 1866 and 1867. He died in Windsor in 1868 after a political career that had spanned three and a half decades of perhaps the most tumultuous and fateful history of the nation.

Whig supremacy lasted little more than a decade in North Carolina. After the election of Van Buren in 1836, Whigs in Bertie responded with majorities for their candidates from 1840 through 1852. The margin of victory, like that in the state, was sometimes narrow, only thirty-six votes in

1844 when Henry Clay bested James K. Polk. And while the county provided a fifty-vote majority for Winfield Scott in 1852, the Democrats in the state managed to triumph with their candidate Franklin Pierce.

After 1852 the national political picture altered quickly and significantly. The Whig party, disrupted by the slavery question, disappeared as a national organization. Some of its adherents, depending upon their views on slavery, gravitated to the Democrats; others joined the newly created Republican party, a reform effort devoted to the antislavery cause. Still others found temporary refuge in the American party, a nativist group that sprang from the anti-Catholic sentiment of the 1840s. Unwilling to support the "Black Republican" party or capitulate to the Democrats, Bertie in 1856 championed the candidate of the American party, former president Millard Fillmore, though North Carolina supported the Democrats.

In 1860 the national political picture was, if anything, more confused than in 1856. While the Republicans offered Abraham Lincoln, the Democrats divided over the slavery issue into northern and southern wings that ran Stephen Douglas and John C. Breckinridge respectively. For those who wanted a compromise candidate, John Bell of the Constitutional Union party provided ephemeral hope. Many Whigs and those who voted the American ticket found refuge there. Hence it was not surprising that Bertie supported Bell, giving him 59 percent of the county's vote, while Breckinridge ran a distant second.

The victor in 1860 was Lincoln. The election of a Republican who represented a party committed to antislavery principles so alarmed South Carolina that a special convention in the state, meeting in December, 1860, decided that secession was the only means by which the state could protect its peculiar institution. Six other southern states joined the secessionist cause and formed the Confederate States of America in 1861.

Despite the decision of its sister states and a vocal secessionist press, North Carolina remained in the Union. Whigs looked askance upon secession, and even many Democrats were only lukewarm in their disunionist sentiments. The legislature that met in late 1860 reflected the divided opinion in the state. Leading the Unionists in that session were P. T. Henry of Bertie in the lower house and David Outlaw in the upper chamber.

Governor John Ellis, however, evidenced sympathy for the secessionists and pressed the legislature to call a convention to consider leaving the Union. After countless resolutions and fruitless debate, the legislature in January, 1861, decided to allow the people in a referendum to be held in February to decide whether to call for a convention that in turn would consider secession. Upon going to the polls the voters would also elect representatives to the convention in case the issue carried in the affirmative.

In the midst of the furor Bertie remained staunchly committed to the United States. Union meetings were held in the county to oppose secession and the convention. Kenneth Rayner wrote sardonically in December, 1860, that he found "that the feeling in Hertford, Bertie, Gates, and adjacent country, was in a great measure in favor of 'the union at any and all hazards'—in other words, unqualified submission." In the referendum North Carolinians by a narrow margin rejected the proposed convention, but Bertie voters cast over 80 percent of their ballots against the proposed meeting. Had the convention met, Bertie would have sent two Unionist representatives, one of only two counties in which slaves constituted a majority of the population to adopt such a stance. Despite the adverse vote throughout the state, secessionist papers like the *Wilmington Journal* remained confident, sure of a reversal, for the "seed is sown and events will develop and ripen their fruits with miraculous speed."

The Wilmington paper forecast accurately. Maintaining their clamor, the secessionists were rewarded by an instant change of opinion after the attack on Fort Sumter, Lincoln's call for troops, and the secession of Virginia. According to Rayner, "This furor, this moral epidemic, swept over the country like a tempest, before which the entire population seemed to succumb." So sure of impending secession was Governor Ellis that he began to make preparations for war, even before the meeting of a special session of the legislature on May 1, 1861.

When the legislature met, Ellis urged adequate defense measures, requested military aid for Virginia, and sought a special convention to translate secessionist spirit into accomplished fact. Acting with alacrity, both houses endorsed the governor's proposals and called for a convention to meet in Raleigh on May 13. P. T. Henry of Bertie voted affirmatively on the convention measure but protested the measure as a "high-handed usurpation of power." Henry objected to the inadequate length of time allowed for campaigning and to the unlimited power of the convention, which effectively prevented the people from approving or rejecting its actions.

Predictably, the convention took North Carolina from the Union, and the state shortly joined the Confederacy. Bertie, like North Carolina, contributed generously to the war effort. At least eight companies, wholly or partly composed of Bertie men, saw service. The pride of the county was Company C of the Eleventh North Carolina Regiment, which succeeded the famed "Bethel Regiment" at a reorganization in Raleigh in 1862. After spending the remainder of the year in guard duty along the North Carolina coast, occasionally battling Union troops in the area, the regiment joined the Pettigrew Brigade in 1863 in time to participate in the Battle of Gettysburg. Suffering heavy losses in the ill-fated campaign, the

Eleventh Regiment spent the remainder of the war in northern Virginia trying to fend off the advances of General Ulysses S. Grant. In April, 1865, Company C, reduced to a Corporal's Guard, surrendered with General Robert E. Lee at Appomattox.

The war and Company C remained indelibly imprinted upon the memories of the people. When the Bertie County Confederate Veterans Association organized in 1889, Captain E. R. Outlaw, Company C, was elected its first president. He also chaired the committee to erect a monument dedicated to the Confederate dead from Bertie. After years of fund raising, "a full sized, well equipped statue of a Confederate soldier" was placed in the courthouse yard. At the unveiling ceremony in August, 1896, John Edward Tyler delivered a poem of commemoration entitled "Bertie at Gettysburg." It was an ode directed principally to the efforts of Company C. Among other verses was the stanza:

> Among the flags it floated high,
>   The flag of the Bertie men;
> Our gallant standard starred and barred,
>   The colors of Company C
>
> Into the struggle went thirty-eight
>   Privates of Company C,
> And on the field when the fight was o'er,
> Dead and wounded lay thirty-four
>   Privates of Company C.

While the Eleventh Regiment and other Bertie soldiers carried the war beyond the state, Federal troops brought the war to North Carolina. By 1862 Union soldiers occupied the coastal regions of the state, and the rivers that bordered and intersected Bertie allowed easy access to the county. Catherine Ann Devereux Edmondston recorded in her diary in January, 1864, that "A party of Yankees" raided Windsor and "committed the usual excesses," kidnapping Cyrus Watson, rector of St. Thomas Episcopal Church, and two other prominent residents of the town, all of whom were subsequently released. Federal troops occupied Windsor again late in the month and in December, 1864, were in the Indian Woods area "committing . . . fearful ravages."

Bertie's soldiers sometimes reflected their preoccupation with the home front. Company F of the Fifty-ninth Regiment, raised mostly in Bertie, had a 33 percent desertion rate. Upon his resignation from the regiment, Joseph J. Watford offered reasons of ill health and the nearness of his estate to enemy lines as an explanation for his departure. Still, the county gave its support to Zebulon B. Vance in the election of 1862, and in 1864 it increased Vance's winning margin to 70 percent of the vote when the governor opposed a peace candidate, William W. Holden.

After the conclusion of their unsuccessful effort to establish their independence, the defeated southern states underwent a dual reconstruction. First they organized governments under directives issued by President Andrew Johnson. A North Carolina constitutional convention in 1865, at which Lewis Thompson and John Pool represented Bertie, provided the basis for a new state government. Bertie, like the state, approved the work of the convention by voting to repeal the ordinance of secession, abolishing slavery, and electing officers for the government.

In Washington, however, the dominant Republican party refused to accept the validity of presidential reconstruction and admit representatives from the former Confederate states to their seats in Congress. Instead, in 1867, the "Radical Republicans" passed legislation over the veto of President Johnson to present their own conception of reconstruction, which depended for implementation upon the United States Army. From the standpoint of most southern whites congressional reconstruction was anathema because it not only attempted to establish the Republican party in the South but also tried to secure civil if not social equality for Negroes. Nonetheless, in 1868 under the watchful eyes of federal troops qualified voters went to the polls to select representatives to another constitutional convention.

Politically, congressional reconstruction marked the triumph of the Republican party in North Carolina, particularly in the eastern "black

John Pool (1826-1884), a Whig, carried Bertie County in the gubernatorial election of 1860 but lost to John W. Ellis. At the state's Constitutional Convention of 1865 Pool represented Bertie County; two years later he helped organize the Republican party in North Carolina. Originally denied a seat in the Senate in 1866, he was again elected to that body in 1868 and served until 1873.

counties," which contained a majority of Negroes whose loyalties were firmly attached to the Republicans. While numerous former Confederates were denied the franchise, blacks for the first time enjoyed the right to vote. Since Negroes supplied the bulk of the Republican vote, the Democrats, or Conservatives as they were often styled, were overwhelmed. Bertie evidenced its newfound Republicanism by approving the 1868 constitution by a two-to-one margin. Later in 1868 the county supported Republicans Ulysses S. Grant and William W. Holden, who became president of the United States and governor of North Carolina respectively.

The triumph of Republicanism in North Carolina proved temporary. The Democrats began their drive to "redeem" the state in 1870 by capturing both houses of the state legislature and by impeaching and removing Governor Holden from office. Still, the Republican lieutenant governor, Tod R. Caldwell, succeeded Holden and was elected to the office in 1872. Grant also carried the state handily that year in his bid for reelection, though the Democrats continued to control the General Assembly. By 1876, however, the Democrats successfully overturned Republican reconstruction when they elected the governor of the state, maintained their dominance in the legislature, and supported Samuel J. Tilden for the presidency.

Nonetheless, the Republicans remained entrenched in North Carolina politics, especially in the "black counties," and the two decades following the advent of congressional reconstruction saw the initial appearance of Negroes in politics. Parker Robbins and Bryant Lee ably represented Bertie in the Constitutional Convention of 1868. The former proceeded to serve two terms in the House of Commons, one of thirty-four Negroes in the North Carolina legislature from 1868 to 1872. During the following decade Augustus Robbins won election to the House of Commons. George A. Mebane, one of the state's outstanding Negro legislators in the last quarter of the century, also came from Bertie. Born of slave parents, Mebane at age thirteen escaped to Union lines during the Civil War. Befriended by an officer, Mebane went north after the war where he was educated in McKean County, Pennsylvania. He returned to Bertie in 1871 to become a schoolteacher but soon moved into politics. He sat in the state Senate on two occasions, 1876-1877 and in 1883.

Despite their minority status the Democrats in Bertie spared no effort to gain control of county politics. In the 1874 campaign the Democratic county convention declared, "We know nothing of those who tyrannize and lord it over us, but misrule, oppression, taxation. Sans Culotteism, rowdyism, drunkenness, incompetency and debauchery, political and personal[,] have full sway in Bertie County." The answer to such degradation

George A. Mebane was born a slave in Bertie County but escaped to Union lines during the Civil War. After being educated in the North, he returned to Bertie in 1871, taught school, and represented the county in the state Senate, 1876-1877 and 1883.

must be organization by the Democrats so that "we shall behold our once happy land, redeemed disenthralled regenerated forever, from the blighting, blasting, withering influence of radicalism and rowdyism."

Although the Democrats scored occasional victories, the Republicans continued to contest county elections successfully. Not until 1888, after a decade of steady exodus by blacks who sought better economic opportunities beyond North Carolina and the passage of discriminatory voting laws by the state legislature, did the Democrats of Bertie finally muster majorities for the party's presidential and gubernatorial candidates. Even then the Republicans remained a potent minority, and blacks still appeared in local and municipal offices.

Ironically, just as the Democrats cemented their hold on Bertie an agrarian reform movement rent the party, once again allowing the Republicans a major voice in political affairs. After 1876 the Democratic party, sometimes tenuously, commanded the political arena in North Carolina with the exception of the fusion period from 1894 to 1901. During that brief interlude the Populist party cooperated with the Republicans to overthrow Democratic rule. Populism originated as a reform effort on the part of economically depressed farmers who desired to improve agricultural conditions. In the South it was largely the political manifestation of the Southern Agricultural Alliance, a farm protest movement organized in the 1880s. The predominantly agrarian populace of

North Carolina and Bertie County naturally inclined the state and county toward a favorable reception to the Alliance and Populism.

Leading the Democrats in the factious politics of the 1890s was Jesse B. Stokes. Although never a man of prominence in state affairs, Stokes chaired the executive committee of the county party and directed local matters from his seat on the board of county commissioners. In effusive praise the *Ledger* characterized Stokes as a "tireless and persistent" individual who had "the brains to plan and the energy and courage to execute." His counterparts in the Populist party were Marcus J. Raynor and James Madison Early, though the latter apparently switched to the Republican party in the late 1890s, an organization in Bertie that was dominated by a Negro politician from Windsor, Ben Askew.

Although Populism made its initial appearance in American politics in 1890 and evidenced considerable strength at the polls two years later, its impact was muted in North Carolina in 1892 by the election of Elias Carr of Edgecombe County, an Allianceman and Democrat, as governor of the state. Nonetheless, Carr achieved a majority of only four votes in Bertie in that election. By 1894 the Populists and Republicans successfully united their efforts by adopting a tactic called "fusion" whereby they won control of the state legislature. In 1896 fusion permitted the election of Daniel Russell, the first Republican governor of the state since Reconstruction, the continued domination of the legislature by Populists and Republicans, and the appearance of Republicans in various county and local offices.

After the advent of fusion, the election of Russell, and the triumph of Republican William McKinley in the presidential contest of 1896, Negroes again appeared in positions of civil and political responsibility in Bertie. Ben Askew became county jailer. Sixteen justices of the peace and eighteen school district committeemen assumed their respective positions. Governor Russell appointed a black notary public, and the McKinley administration entrusted at least seven Bertie post offices to black postmasters and postmistresses. And representing the Second Congressional District of which Bertie was a part was George H. White, a native of Edgecombe County and one of the most distinguished Negro legislators in Washington, D.C., in the closing years of the nineteenth century.

Briefly impinging upon the local political struggle was the Spanish-American War of 1898, which found substantial support in Bertie. As early as 1895, when Cuban rebels staged another of their many uprisings against Spanish governments, the *Windsor Ledger* compared them to America revolutionaries. "Let Cuba be free!" demanded the newspaper. As the United States considered a declaration of war in 1898, a writer from the

Sans Souci area declared that the country owed assistance to those who suffered "the most terrible agonies at the hands of Spanish despotism."

After the decision for war in April, Alex Lassiter announced that he had received permission from the state's governor to raise a company of volunteers for the Third North Carolina Regiment. By July seven Bertie men had joined, though they served in the Edgecombe Guard, Company I. Although the county enlistees never participated in the conflict in Cuba, Bertie supported the principle of intervention for the purpose of furthering the cause of freedom. At the same time it opposed the annexation of Hawaii in 1898 and other evidences of imperialism that derived from the victory in the Spanish-American War as contrary to the principle of freedom and the policy of the founders of the American nation.

Approval of efforts by oppressed Cubans to throw off the yoke of Spanish colonialism failed to translate into political tolerance for Populists and Negroes at home in Bertie County. While disparate economic interests and social distinctions divided the white populace, a sense of racial superiority and hence racial solidarity served as a basis of agreement to unite most whites. Upon that basis the Democrats moved to challenge the Populists and Republicans. White government clubs and the blatant use of racism mocked the democratic process. The electoral results heartened the Democrats. In very close races party candidates captured the local offices of sheriff, clerk of court, register of deeds, coroner, and surveyor. The party also gained control of the board of county commissioners and sent Francis D. Winston to the state House of Representatives.

Although the Populist-Republican hold on the county had been broken, white supremacy and Democratic domination had not been fully realized. Republican congressman George H. White won reelection to the House of Representatives while the Democratic nominee for the Bertie state Senate seat lost to his Republican opponent. Locally, the three magistrates and constable of Woodsville Township and the two magistrates and constable of Indian Woods Township were Negroes. In Snakebite Township two justices and the constable were Populists; the third justice was a Negro. And blacks also remained on the county school board.

While Jesse B. Stokes led the Democrats in Bertie, the county's most outstanding and influential leader in state politics was Francis D. Winston. Born in 1857 into the distinguished Winston family of Bertie, Frank Winston attended Cornell University and the University of North Carolina, being graduated from the latter in 1879. He studied law, obtained a license to practice in 1881, and enjoyed a successful legal career in Windsor. His entree into politics came via his appointment as clerk of the county court in 1881. He later represented the county in the state Senate in 1887 and in the lower house in 1899 where he was a leader in

Francis D. Winston had an unusual career. He entered politics as a Republican, cooperated with Negroes in the GOP like George H. White, and then in the 1890s switched to the Democratic party. As a Democrat, he helped organize the violent white supremacy campaigns of 1898 and 1900 and in the 1899 legislature introduced the suffrage bill that disfranchised black voters. From Josephus Daniels, *Editor in Politics* (Chapel Hill: University of North Carolina Press, 1941), opposite p. 298.

the Democratic ranks. After a brief career on the bench that began in 1901 when he was appointed judge of the Second Judicial District of North Carolina, Winston served as lieutenant governor of the state from 1905 to 1909.

Winston was one of the foremost advocates of "white supremacy" in the state. It was he who suggested the formation of what were called "white supremacy clubs," though he referred to them as "White government unions," in 1898 to appeal to race loyalty and engender support for the Democrats. Following his election to the state house, Winston, in 1899, presented the first suffrage bill in the legislature that was designed to disfranchise blacks. Patterned after a similar Louisiana statute, the bill used educational and property qualifications to discriminate against blacks but resorted to a "grandfather clause" to protect the voting rights of illiterate and poor whites. Winston's bill became the basis of the famed discriminatory suffrage amendment approved by the legislature and placed before the people in the August, 1900, general election.

The Democrats planned diligently to renew and enlarge upon their success in 1898 with victories in 1900. Again the emphasis was on race, with the intention that whites would manage the affairs of the county. The *Windsor Ledger* editorialized, let "manhood determine to install white supremacy forever or die. . . . " Even a lifelong white Republican agreed that his race pride and self-respect demanded that he vote for the suffrage amendment. And the *Ledger* followed with the admonition: "every self-respecting white man" must work to carry the county for "white folks and decent government." Whites, "the guardians of virtue, intelligence, property and race pride of the county," must permit nothing to prevent their success.

In early spring Democrats, Republicans, and Populists held their county conventions, but the Democrats controlled the momentum of the course of political events. White supremacy clubs continued to appear in the towns and crossroads communities. Mass meetings were organized by which the Democratic leaders exhorted their following. A particularly elaborate and lavish gathering occurred in Windsor on May 30, featuring delegates from the county and surrounding areas, a parade that included male and female participants and the Windsor Naval Reserve, singing, and speech making. The color line was drawn and whites were reminded to remember whites who voted against the suffrage amendment as alien to their own civilization and persons deserving social and economic ostracism. The question clearly was "Shall the White Man Rule?"

Organization, intimidation, and determination rewarded the Democrats in Bertie with victory on the suffrage issue. Every township provided a majority in favor of the amendment; and the county's majority, 2,649 to 944, by a three-to-one margin assisted the ratification of the amendment throughout the state. With crushing decisiveness the Democratic party swept the county and state. In Bertie the Republican gubernatorial candidate captured only 27 percent of the ballots, and in November McKinley received 644 fewer votes than in 1896.

The suffrage amendment accomplished its purpose. The black vote declined substantially, and coupled with the obvious determination of whites to dominate politics, Negro participation in politics diminished to nugatory importance. The last casualty in the realm of Bertie politics was Congressman George White, who left Washington in 1901, the last black to sit in Congress for almost three decades. Ironically, one-time Republican Francis D. Winston, responsible for the "white supremacy clubs" and originator of the suffrage amendment, had written White in 1890 when the congressman had been solicitor and prosecuting attorney for the Second Judicial District, apologizing to White for being unable to attend the state judicial convention, asking White to secure his nomination for a judgeship, stating that riding the circuit with him would be "a great pleasure," and wishing White success in his endeavors.

After 1900 Bertie remained firmly wedded to the Democratic party for more than half a century. While United States senatorial and state gubernatorial candidates counted upon more than 90 percent of the vote in the county, presidential candidates polled over 80 percent of the ballots.

Neither Republicans nor third-party hopefuls met encouragement in the county until 1968. Bull Moose candidate Theodore Roosevelt received sixty-one votes in 1912. In 1948 Progressive party candidate, Henry Wallace, and Strom Thurmond, Dixiecrat, obtained four and forty-seven votes respectively.

The 1960s, a decade characterized by civil violence and the prosecution of the unpopular Vietnam War by Democratic presidents, unsettled politics in the nation, state, and county. In 1968 the American Independent party, headed by Governor George Wallace of Alabama, appealed to those of conservative persuasion and particularly to those frightened by the civil rights movement of the past decade. The liberal Democratic candidate for the presidency, Hubert H. Humphrey from Minnesota, polled a plurality of only 45 percent of Bertie's votes. Wallace followed closely with 43.6 percent of the ballots.

The Democrats continued to experience adversity in 1972. When the party nominated George McGovern, a confirmed liberal from South Dakota, Bertie and North Carolina turned to the Republican candidate, Richard M. Nixon. The overwhelming majority polled by Nixon in the state probably helped Republican James Holshouser capture the gubernatorial contest that year. Although Holshouser failed to carry Bertie, his 31 percent of the vote in the county represented the best showing of a Republican candidate for governor since Daniel Russell in 1896.

Fundamentally, the county remained Democratic, however, and the 1968 and 1972 elections proved aberrations from the normal course of politics. The Democratic senatorial candidate in 1974 won 90 percent of the Bertie vote, and in 1976 the Democratic party dominated the scene. Presidential candidate Jimmy Carter from Georgia tallied three fourths of the Bertie ballots; gubernatorial candidate James Hunt scored an even more resounding victory. The Democrats continued their success in 1980, scoring huge majorities in the county for their presidential, gubernatorial, and senatorial candidates, Carter, Hunt, and Robert Morgan, respectively. Although the Republican party can successfully contest presidential and gubernatorial races in North Carolina, the Democrats appear firmly entrenched in Bertie, and party candidates should expect to dominate the county's politics in the foreseeable future.

BIBLIOGRAPHICAL ESSAY

No satisfactory history of Bertie County is available, though a number of secondary accounts offer insights into various aspects of the county's past. Such works include the studies of John Tyler, particularly his *Bertie County's Colonial and State Governors* (Roxobel[?]: Privately printed, 1950), Bill Sharpe, *A New Geography of North Carolina* (Raleigh: Sharpe Publishing Co., 4 volumes, 1954-1965), IV, 1713-1736, and Edward A. Terry, *County Government and County Affairs in Bertie County* (Chapel Hill: University of North Carolina Press, 1929). Also helpful are *Bertie County, North Carolina: An Economic Study*, produced by Virginia Electric and Power Company in 1965, and *Bertie County and Land Development Plan*, provided by Coastal Area Management Association in 1976.

Currently, primary source materials must form the basis of any extended and reliable understanding of Bertie's history. For the eighteenth century *The Colonial Records of North Carolina*, edited by William L. Saunders (Raleigh: State of North Carolina, 10 volumes, 1886-1890), and *The State Records of North Carolina*, edited by Walter Clark (Winston and Goldsboro: State of North Carolina, 16 volumes, 1895-1906), are indispensable. Newspapers, particularly those of Windsor but also those of neighboring towns such as Edenton, are immensely instructive. Of great importance is the vast collection of county records housed in the State Archives in Raleigh, North Carolina. And not to be overlooked are the manuscript collections in the State Archives and more especially in the Southern Historical Collection in Chapel Hill, North Carolina, where the William D. Valentine Diaries, the William R. Capehart Papers, the Stephen A. Norfleet Diaries, and the Francis D. Winston Papers prove illuminating.